THE WHITE HART LANE ENCYCLOPEDIA

An A-Z of Tottenham Hotspur

Other titles available in the same series
The Anfield Encyclopedia: an A–Z of Liverpool FC
The Old Trafford Encyclopedia: an A–Z of Manchester United FC
The Highbury Encyclopedia: an A–Z of Arsenal FC
The Elland Road Encyclopedia: an A–Z of Leeds United FC
The Stamford Bridge Encyclopedia: an A–Z of Chelsea FC
The Maine Road Encyclopedia: an A–Z of Manchester City FC
The White Hart Lane Encyclopedia: an A–Z of Tottenham Hotspur FC
The St James's Park Encyclopedia: an A–Z of Newcastle United FC
The Hawthorns Encyclopedia; an A–Z of West Bromwich Albion FC

All the photographs have been supplied by Les Gold Promotions and the author is grateful to Les Gold for his permission to reproduce them in this book

THE
WHITE HART LANE
ENCYCLOPEDIA

**An A-Z of
Tottenham
Hotspur FC**

Paul Harrison

MAINSTREAM
PUBLISHING

EDINBURGH AND LONDON

For Elaine, Andrew and Carla with thanks for their help,
patience and encouragement.

First published in Great Britain in 1996 by
MAINSTREAM PUBLISHING COMPANY (EDINBURGH) LTD
7 Albany Street
Edinburgh EH1 3UG

ISBN 1 85158 802 7

Typeset in 11/13pt Janson
Printed and bound in Great Britain by The Cromwell Press, Melksham

ABANDONED MATCHES. A match which is called off by the
referee, whilst it is in progress, because conditions do not permit
it to be completed. Generally speaking, far fewer matches are now
abandoned because if there is some doubt about the ability to play
the full game, the match is more likely to be postponed. In the
second round of the 1903–04 FA Cup, Spurs placed seats inside
the fence to increase the capacity of the ground for their match
against Aston Villa. At half-time many sitting in these seats invaded the pitch and were followed by hundreds of others from the
stands. As they refused to go back, the referee abandoned the
game. The crowd on the pitch started to demonstrate and the
police had to move in to avoid a riot. The match was replayed at
Villa Park and Spurs were fined £350.

AGGREGATE SCORE. Tottenham's highest aggregate score in
any competition came in the UEFA Cup in September 1971
against Keflavik of Iceland, when they notched up 15 goals over
two legs. Spurs won the first leg in Iceland 6–1 and then 9–0 at
White Hart Lane.

ALEKSIC, MILIJA. Born of a Yugoslavian father at Newcastle-
under-Lyme in Staffordshire, he first came to prominence when
he helped Stafford Rangers win the FA Trophy in 1972. His entry

into the Football League came the following season with Plymouth Argyle. While at Home Park he went to Ipswich and Oxford on loan before signing for Luton Town in December 1976. Two years later, Keith Burkinshaw paid out £100,000 for the goalkeeper nicknamed 'Elastic'. After only two matches he was injured and in 1980 he broke his jaw in a collision with Joe Jordan in an FA Cup replay at Old Trafford. Ironically, it was an injury to Barry Daines which allowed him to return to the first team. He seized the opportunity so well that he retained his place for both FA Cup final clashes with Manchester City. In August 1981, Spurs signed Ray Clemence from Liverpool and his opportunities became restricted. He left White Hart Lane in the summer of 1982 to take up coaching in South Africa.

ALLEN, CLIVE. Although Clive was not to win as many trophies as his father Les, he did achieve the distinction of scoring more competitive goals in a season than anybody else when he scored an amazing total of 49 goals (33 Football League, plus 16 in the two Cup competitions) in 1986–87. Starting out with Queen's Park Rangers, he made his Football League debut against Chelsea in November 1978 and after scoring in his fourth substitute appearance, he grabbed a hat-trick in his first full match, a 5–1 victory at Coventry City on 28 April 1979. After top-scoring for Rangers with 28 Football League goals from 39 Second Division appearances the following season, he was signed by Arsenal for £1.25 million in June 1980, but passed on to Crystal Palace before the new season even started, in part-exchange for Kenny Sansom. Despite a good start at Selhurst Park with a hat-trick in his third game, he didn't settle and returned to Queen's Park Rangers in the summer of 1981. After impressing towards the end of the 1983–84 season, he was included in Bobby Robson's England squad for the South American tour and made his full England debut against Brazil in June 1984. That summer he joined Tottenham Hotspur, but in each of his first two seasons at White Hart Lane his appearances were restricted by injury. It was only in 1986–87 when operating as a lone striker that he showed the full depth of his clinical finishing with those 49 goals, as Spurs finished third in the League and reached the FA Cup final where they lost 3–2 to Coventry City. He was voted Player of the Year in the annual PFA awards and Footballer of the Year by the

Clive Allen

Football Writers' Association. He was also recalled to the England side but failed to impress in a 0–0 draw with Turkey. At the end of the following season he signed for French champions Bordeaux, but after only one season he returned to England to sign for Manchester City. Moving to Chelsea in December 1991 he became an immediate favourite with the fans, but not with Ian Porterfield, who sold him on to West Ham United. In March 1994, he joined Millwall in a £75,000 deal.

ALLEN, LES. Signed from Chelsea in part-exchange for England international Johnny Brooks, Les Allen proved a prolific goalscorer and instinctive inside the penalty area. Although he did not score on his debut, he scored two in his next match and, a few weeks later, five in a 13–2 FA Cup replay defeat of Crewe Alexandra. He was an ever-present in the 'double' winning team of 1960–61, scoring 27 League and Cup goals. He was capped for England Under-23s and represented the Football League side that played the Italian League in November 1962. The arrival of Jimmy Greaves was expected to mark the end of his days at White Hart Lane, but in fact he competed with Bobby Smith for the centre-forward spot and it wasn't until Alan Gilzean joined the Club in December 1964 that he slipped out of contention. The following summer he moved to Queen's Park Rangers in a £21,000 deal. At Loftus Road he won a League Cup winners' medal and helped their rise from the third to the First Division. In December 1968 he was appointed Rangers' manager but only held the post until January 1971. He later returned to League management with Swindon Town.

ALLEN, PAUL. The third member of the footballing Allen family to play for Spurs, he learnt his trade at the West Ham United 'Academy' before making his Football League debut at home to Burnley as the youngest player ever to turn out for the Hammers on 29 September 1979. He went on to play in 31 matches that season as well as making history by being the youngest player at 17 years 256 days to appear in an FA Cup final when West Ham beat Arsenal 1–0. By the summer of 1985 he had added England Under-21 honours to his record 23 youth caps. He signed for Tottenham for a fee of £400,000 (decided by a tribunal) and his cousin Clive was among his new team-mates. Initially all went well as he scored on his debut at home to Watford, but soon his form dipped as he strove hard to fit into the Spurs set-up. He played in the 1987 FA Cup final and was an ever-present in 1991 when Spurs beat Nottingham Forest 2–1 in extra-time to win the trophy for the eighth time. A player with a tremendous work-rate, he always seemed to pop up with the odd goal to underline his great value to the side. He left White Hart Lane in September 1993 to join Southampton for a £550,000 fee.

ALL-LONDON FINAL. The first all-London Cup final was on 20 May 1967 when Tottenham Hotspur beat Chelsea 2–1 on a wet and slippery pitch, although the game itself was played in sunshine. Robertson scored the first goal for Spurs just before half-time and Saul their second in the 68th minute. Tambling headed in for Chelsea with five minutes left but it was too late to affect the result.

ALMOND, WILLIE. Joining Blackburn Rovers in 1888 for the first season of League football, he became a regular member of the Rovers team of the late 1880s and early 1890s before signing for Accrington. He then spent a year with both Middlesbrough and Millwall Athletic before joining Spurs for the 1895–96 season. When Spurs adopted professionalism, Almond continued to play as an amateur which allowed him to turn out for Clapton and Millwall during his two years at Spurs.

ALSFORD, WALLY. A wing-half who could also play at centre-half or inside-forward, he joined the White Hart Lane staff in August 1930 and made his debut on 27 October in a London FA Charity Cup tie against Chelsea. Not always able to establish himself as a first-team regular, his best season with the club was 1934–35 when he won an England cap against Scotland, but unfortunately the club was relegated! He later joined Nottingham Forest but within 12 months was found to be suffering from osteomyelitis, a bone marrow inflammation, and was told he would never play again. He retired in May 1938 but did in fact turn out for Forest and guested for several other clubs during the Second World War.

AMBLER, CHARLIE. Born with the surname of Toby, Charlie Ambler joined Spurs from Luton Town in October 1894. He quickly established himself as the club's first choice 'keeper but as Spurs were not at the time competing in any organised League competition, he was free to play for other clubs. In November 1895 he played one Football League game for Woolwich Arsenal. One of London's best goalkeepers, Ambler won a number of representative honours as a Spurs player.

ANDERSON, JIMMY. Joining Spurs as a ground staff boy in 1908, Jimmy Anderson did a variety of jobs at White Hart Lane until being appointed manager in 1955. He already knew the players well and if a little old for the job, he was a perfect stop-gap whilst player-coach Bill Nicholson was being groomed for the manager's position.

ANDERTON, DARREN. Brilliant winger who hit the headlines during Portsmouth's long FA Cup run of 1991–92. In fact, he showed such good form that he was the subject of transfer speculation even before the club started its FA Cup run. Scored both goals in Portsmouth's fourth-round victory over Leyton Orient and another couple in the club's 4–2 win over Middlesbrough at Ayresome Park. In the semi-final he scored a breakaway goal in extra-time against Liverpool which seemed certain to take Portsmouth to Wembley, until the Reds' last-gasp equaliser. He signed for Spurs in May 1992 for £1.75 million. Initially, he struggled to regain the form that prompted the club to buy him but since then he has not been absent from the team, save for injury, and his excellent performances warranted a call-up to the full England team.

ANGELS. The three angels of Tottenham Hotspur are traditionally supposed to bring the team good luck – an example of enduring football superstition, the role of the three angels is often portrayed by supporters in fancy dress. Three is also considered a lucky number for the club.

ANGLO-ITALIAN LEAGUE CUP. An annual match between the winners of the Football League Cup and Italian Cup. The League Cup winners were not guaranteed European football at the time, but once they gained automatic entry into the UEFA Cup in 1972, the competition ceased. In September 1971, Spurs played AC Torino over two legs, winning 1–0 in Italy and 2–0 at White Hart Lane.

APPEARANCES. Steve Perryman holds the record for the greatest number of appearances in a Tottenham shirt, with a total of 852 games to his credit between 1969 and 1986. In all, Perryman played 654 League games, 69 FA Cup games, 65 Football League Cup games and 63 European matches. He also made a number of appearances as a substitute.

ARCHIBALD, STEVE. A member of Clyde's 1978 Scottish Second Division winning team, he joined Aberdeen for £25,000 and scored 23 goals in 1979–80 to help Dons with the Scottish Premier Division championship. He moved to Tottenham in May

1980 for £800,000 – the fee being a record for a transfer between Scottish and English clubs. Forming a partnership with Garth Crooks, who was signed from Stoke City to partner him up front, his thirst for goals made him a great favourite of Spurs fans. He led the attack in both the 1981 and 1982 FA Cup finals and scored Spurs' goal in the 1982 Football League Cup final. Whilst at White Hart Lane he added 22 Scottish caps to the one he had won whilst with Aberdeen. In August 1984, following a well-publicised rift with Keith Burkinshaw, he was transferred to Barcelona for £1.5 million. In his first season they won the Spanish League and the following year reached the European Cup final. Four more Scottish caps were won, but with the signings of Mark Hughes and Gary Lineker, he was allowed to leave midway through the 1987–88 season to join Blackburn Rovers on loan. At the end of the season he was released and joined Hibernian, but in January 1990 he bought up his own contract and returned to Spain to play for Second Division Espanol. Ten months later he returned to Scotland to play for St Mirren and later Ayr United.

ARDILES, OSVALDO. A midfield dynamo, his short-passing was a delight to watch and although only small in frame, he was a terrier in the midfield, giving his opponents little time to dwell on the ball. He sprang to prominence in 1978 when he displayed his superb abilities for Argentina in the World Cup finals. He was signed from Huracan of Buenos Aires for £325,000 by manager Keith Burkinshaw and Spurs won the FA Cup twice and also gained the UEFA Cup with Ardiles in their ranks. By the time of his first English club honour, a 1981 FA Cup winners' medal, he was beloved of the Spurs supporters and the marketing of the Spurs pop record Ossie's Dream revolved around him. He had to miss the 1982 FA Cup final because of the Falklands conflict and moved on to Paris St Germain on loan until the animosity against Argentina subsided. Then began a series of injuries that was to plague him for more than three years. He was honoured with a benefit match against Inter Milan in May 1986 and many thought this was the time for him to retire. However, he was back to his best the following season and he appeared in the 1987 FA Cup final defeat by Coventry City. In August of that year he played as substitute for the Football League in the Centenary Celebration match against the Rest of the World and the following month

Osvaldo Ardiles

captained the League side against the Irish League in Belfast. He joined Blackburn Rovers on loan in 1987–88 but injuries prevented him from playing much of a role in their push for promotion from the Second Division. Given a free transfer by Spurs he joined Queen's Park Rangers but a broken leg limited his appearances. In July 1989 he became manager of Swindon Town and completely transformed their style of play. They won the Second Division play-offs in 1989–90 but were denied their place in the First Division after an illegal payments scandal at the club. In March 1991 he took over as manager of struggling Newcastle United but was sacked as the Magpies faced the possibility of relegation to Division Three for the first time in their history. It was not long before he was made manager of West Bromwich Albion and under his guidance in 1993 they gained promotion to the First Division via the play-offs. Then Ardiles controversially quit to take over at Tottenham Hotspur. Even though he produced a masterstroke in securing the signature of Jürgen Klinsmann, not enough games were being won and in November 1994, amid tense speculation, Ardiles was dismissed.

ARMSTRONG, CHRIS. Newcastle-born, he started his Football League career with Wrexham, but in August 1991 joined Millwall for £50,000. After some impressive performances for the Lions, he signed for Crystal Palace 13 months later for £1 million. He ended his first season with the Eagles as their top scorer with 15 goals but it was not enough to save them from relegation. The following season he emerged as the club's bright star with eight goals in the opening ten games and ended the campaign as top scorer with 23 League goals. The 1994–95 season was one of controversy for Armstrong, because he was banned for having proved positive in a drugs test. When he returned he was in rich scoring form. At the end of the season he joined Spurs for £4.5 million, the club's record fee for an incoming player.

ARMSTRONG, GERRY. Crossing the Irish Sea to join Tottenham in 1975, he spent the following season quite successfully in the reserves, scoring ten goals in 24 Football Combination matches and made his first-team debut in Joe Kinnear's testimonial match. For the next three seasons he vied for one of the central striking positions with John Duncan, Chris Jones, Colin Lee and Ian Moores without ever establishing himself as first choice. One of the game's best-loved and most genuine players, his style was based on hard work and direct running. With the arrival of Steve Archibald and Garth Crooks in the summer of 1980, it came as no surprise when he joined Watford for £250,000. Having made his international debut for Northern Ireland in 1977 he travelled to Spain for the 1982 World Cup. His exploits in the competition, including the winning goal against Spain, earned him an award as British Player of the Tournament. He left such an impression with the host nation's clubs that a year later he joined Real Mallorca. He spent two years in Spain before returning to these shores and spells at West Bromwich Albion, Chesterfield and Brighton.

ATTENDANCE – HIGHEST. The record attendance at White Hart Lane is 75,038 for the sixth round FA Cup game with Sunderland on 5 March 1938. Spurs lost 1–0. The record attendance for a Football League match was on 22 September 1951 when 70,882 watched Spurs beat Manchester United 2–0 with goals from Bennett and Medley.

AWAY MATCHES. Spurs' best away wins have come in the FA Cup when they won 6–0 at Oldham Athletic in 1932–33 and at Margate in 1972–73. The club's best away win in the Football League is 6–1, a scoreline that occurred at Stoke City in 1951–52 and at West Ham United in 1962–63. Spurs' worst defeat away from home is the 8–2 thrashing handed out by Derby County on 16 October 1976. The highest scoring away match Spurs were involved in came in 1914–15 when they went down 7–5 to Middlesbrough.

AWAY SEASONS. The club's highest number of away wins came in 1960–61 when they won 16 of their 21 matches when winning the First Division championship. That 'double' winning season also saw them score 50 goals away from White Hart Lane. Spurs ' fewest away wins (one) occurred in seasons 1909–10, 1914–15, 1928–29 and 1964–65.

B

BAILY, EDDIE. One of the most important names in Spurs' post-war history, first as a player, later as assistant manager to Bill Nicholson. Known affectionately as 'The Cheeky Chappie', he was a key link in the 'push and run' team. One of the game's finest inside-forwards, he was capped for England on nine occasions, scoring five goals in his first five internationals. He also appeared for the Rest of the United Kingdom against Wales and played for the Football League five times. In 1957 he was still considered good enough to play for an England team against Young England. A chirpy Cockney character, he was also an off-the-field personality – even Alf Ramsey was forced to comment on Baily's humour in his autobiography. Ten years after making his Spurs debut in a Football League South match in 1946 he was allowed to move to Port Vale for £6,000, but after only nine months, joined Nottingham Forest, whom he helped gain promotion to the First Division. He ended his playing career with Leyton Orient before returning to White Hart Lane in October 1963. He remained with the club for 11 years as Bill Nicholson's assistant before leaving the club again following Nicholson's resignation.

BAKER, PETER. First spotted by Spurs whilst playing for Enfield, he had already won English youth honours when he signed for Spurs as an amateur. Turning professional in September 1952, he made his League debut that season in a 1–1 draw at Sunderland. He then understudied Alf Ramsey for the next two seasons but his chance of becoming the long-term replacement for the future England manager seemed to disappear with the signing of Maurice Norman from Norwich City. However, injury to Norman early in 1956–57 allowed him to claim the right-back position. A good, positional player, he formed an exceptionally reliable full-back partnership with Ron Henry. He played right-back in the 1961 'double' team. He won an FA Cup winners' medal the following season and a European Cup-winners' Cup medal in 1963. He never quite achieved the stardom of his Spurs colleagues and at international level was very unfortunate in being unable to displace Blackpool's Jimmy Armstrong from the England team. Probably the best all-round sportsman at the club, he was eventually replaced by Cyril Knowles as Bill Nicholson sought to rebuild. In May 1965, his contract was cancelled by mutual consent and he left to join Durban City as player-boss, before embarking on a successful business career in South Africa.

BANKS, JIMMY. Jimmy Banks signed for Spurs from Willington Athletic in the summer of 1913. When war arrived he joined the services but because he was not posted abroad, he was able to turn out regularly in the London Football Combination. During the latter years of World War One he proved very successful as a high-scoring centre-forward. He played in 18 games during the club's Second Division championship season of 1919–20 and the signing of Jimmy Seed added further competition for places. However, in 1921, Fanny Walden was injured and Banks was reinstated at outside-right. A strong, resolute player, his style played an important role in helping Spurs win the FA Cup in 1921. Unable to retain his place early the following season, he moved to Norwich City before finishing his career with Luton Town.

BARMBY, NICK. The son of the old Hull City player, Jeff Barmby, he joined Tottenham Hotspur in March 1990 before turning professional early the next year, having spent some time at the Lilleshall Centre of Excellence. He made his competitive debut at Sheffield Wednesday in September 1992 and coming on as a substitute against Middlesbrough in his first home game, scored a late equaliser. He caused a club versus country row when he was selected for the England Youth side competing in the World Cup finals in Australia. Even though Tottenham wanted him to stay and help them during their FA Cup campaign, the FA got their way and he went to Australia. After helping England to third place, he returned to Spurs in time for their losing FA Cup semi-final against Arsenal. One of the most outstanding English talents of his generation he was surprisingly allowed to join Premier League new boys Middlesbrough in the summer of 1995.

BEAL, PHIL. One of the most loyal players ever to appear on Spurs' books, he made his senior debut deputising at right-half for Danny Blanchflower at Aston Villa in 1963. The arrival of Alan Mullery seemed to leave him in the cold, but his reliable performances, cool head under pressure and a willingness to occupy any of the defensive positions could not be ignored and by early 1967 he was well established. However, a broken arm put him out for the rest of the season, costing him an FA Cup final appearance against Chelsea and, when he was fit to return, he found stiff opposition for the right-back spot from Joe Kinnear. His versatility allowed him to re-establish himself in a tight-marking central defensive role and it was in that position that he played in both the 1971 and the 1973 League Cup finals, the UEFA Cup winning side of 1972 and the losing team in the same 1974 competition. First and foremost a defender, he only scored one goal, but a memorable one it was; picking up the ball deep in his own half, he ran some 75 yards and completed a slick one-two interchange with Jimmy Greaves before cracking the ball home off the cross bar from the edge of the Queen's Park Rangers penalty area. He was awarded a testimonial against Bayern Munich but it was reported that he lost money on the night because of the large fee agreed with the German side. In the summer of 1975 he moved to Brighton and Hove Albion but played only ten games before moving on to American team Memphis Rogues and then Crewe Alexandra.

BELLAMY, WALTER. Associated with Spurs as an amateur for a number of years before turning professional, he played for Dulwich Hamlet, where he won several England caps. His first-team debut came in September 1926 when he played in a London FA Charity Cup tie but he had to wait until the end of the season before making his League debut. Having to compete with Jimmy Dimmock and Willie Evans, he rarely managed to get a lengthy run in the first team in his eight years with the club. He later spent one season with Brighton and Hove Albion.

BENNETT, LES. His first senior game for the club saw him score a hat-trick against Watford in a wartime League match as Spurs won 8–2. During World War Two he served in Egypt, India and Burma and was only able to turn out for Spurs on rare occasions, but he guested for Distillery while on duty in Northern Ireland and even represented the Northern Ireland League XI against the League of Ireland. On being demobbed he went straight into the Spurs team as first choice inside-right, but the hostilities meant he was almost 29 when he made his Football League debut against Birmingham City in August 1946. One of three uncapped players in the side that won the League championship in 1950–51, he had a clever turn and deceptive dribble and was very difficult to mark. One of only eight players to score over 100 League goals for Spurs , he was allowed to join West Ham United in December 1954. He spent just one season at Upton Park, including a spell as captain before joining Romford and later Clacton Town, where he was manager.

BERGSSON, GUDNI. Rejected by Aston Villa after failing to impress in a trial in October 1985, the Icelandic international was a law student when invited to join Spurs on trial some three years later. A utility man who can play at full-back and in midfield, but is at his best sweeping alongside the centre-half, he became a vital member of the first-team squad. His most settled spell was 1991–92 but with the signings of Neil Ruddock, Dean Austin and Jason Cundy and the foreign player ruling being tightened up, it seemed that his future lay away from White Hart Lane. So it was, for in March 1995 he joined Bolton Wanderers for £65,000.

BEST STARTS. Spurs were unbeaten for the first 16 games of the 1960–61 'double' season, when they had 11 straight wins before drawing with Manchester City (home 1–1). They won their next four matches before losing 2–1 at Sheffield Wednesday on 12 November 1960.

BLACK, DAVID. A speedy winger who knew where the goal was, David Black was a huge success at Northumberland Park, missing only three competitive matches of the 1897–98 season. Signed from Burnley to replace Richard McElhaney he showed great strength and resilience as opposition full-backs would mete out rough treatment to dangerous players. After just one season he moved to Woolwich Arsenal but after failing to establish himself he joined Clyde.

BLAIR, JOHN. Though he had only 18 months experience of senior football, Spurs decided to invest in his talent, following an outstanding season for Third Lanark in 1925–26. He scored nine goals in his first 11 League games for Spurs before being sidelined by injury. He managed to get back in the team early the following season and though he scored a hat-trick in a 4–1 home win over Middlesbrough, he could not hold on to his place and in November 1927 he moved to Sheffield United.

BLANCHFLOWER, DANNY. One of the most famous players in Spurs' history and not because he captained the club to its greatest ever triumph of the League and Cup double, but because he was one of the greatest attacking wing-halves of all time. Born in Belfast with the Christian names Robert Denis, he somehow became known as Danny to everyone. As a child Blanchflower was an all-round sportsman who played football for his school sides and the local Boys' Brigade. He studied at Belfast Technical College and was an apprentice engineer for a while. In 1939 he formed his own club called Bloomfield United and so successful was it that he eventually founded a complete league competition. In the war, Danny volunteered for the RAF. He had won a scholarship to St Andrews University and was not called up until he had completed his studies in 1944. During Christmas 1945 he returned to Ireland and signed professional forms for Glentoran. In 1947 he played for the Irish League against the Football League at Goodison Park and impressed many people; this led to a move to Barnsley in April 1949 for a £6,500 fee. Just six months later he made his international debut against Scotland at Windsor Park, but the Irish lost 8–2. In March 1951 he moved to Aston Villa for £15,000 and made his debut on St Patrick's Day in a 3–2 victory over Burnley. As at Barnsley, his intellectual approach to

Danny Blanchflower

the game and his passion for trying new ideas met with resistance and in December 1954 he joined Spurs for a fee of £30,000. Succeeding Alf Ramsey as captain, he fell out with manager Jimmy Anderson after taking it upon himself to change the team pattern during the match without the consent of Anderson. Spurs lost and Danny got the blame and was dropped. When Bill Nicholson became manager he was reinstated as captain. It was not long before Spurs were the supreme team in English football. He captained the side to the League and Cup double in 1960–61, the first time it had been achieved this century. He also scored from a penalty in the Cup final victory over Burnley the following year, sending 'keeper Adam Blacklaw the wrong way from the spot. He was voted Footballer of the Year in both 1958 and 1961 and once in the Irish side he played in 56 out of 62 internationals, including 41 on the trot. They reached the quarter-finals of the 1958 World Cup, having beaten Czechoslovakia 3–2 with a team that had been hit by injuries. His playing career came to an end at Old Trafford in April 1964. After a poor display he was dropped. Not wanting reserve football he decided to retire. A witty, rational and intelligent man, he started a career as a journalist for the *Sunday Express*. He also created a stir when he refused to appear on the *This Is Your Life* television programme, considering it a great invasion of his privacy. He made a brief excursion into football management in December 1978 when he took charge of Chelsea but resigned after nine months. An inspirational player he will always be adored by Spurs fans who supported the club in the 1960s.

BLISS, BERT. Signed from Willenhall Swifts in April 1912, he was a confident shoot-on-sight player and in the season before World War One and the two seasons immediately after the hostilities, Bert Bliss was Spurs' leading goalscorer. In fact, when he returned from the war with receding hair he looked little like a footballer, but in 1919–20 he was an ever-present as Spurs won the Second Division championship. During that campaign he scored 31 goals, many of them with a 'blistering' shot. Although he did not score in the 1921 FA Cup final, his two goals in the semi-final saw off Preston North End. In his one international appearance he must have felt at home, as team-mates Dimmock, Grimsdell and Bert Smith played alongside him. By December 1922 his power was beginning to wane and he was transferred to Clapton Orient before finishing his career with Bournemouth.

BOOKS. Among the many books that have been written about Tottenham Hotspur Football Club are:
Spurs : A Complete Record, Bob Goodwin
Tottenham Hotspur Greats, Harry Harris
Who's Who of Tottenham Hotspur FC, Bob Goodwin
Tottenham Hotspur FC, Fred Ward
Spurs : A History of Tottenham Hotspur FC, Julian Holland
The Tottenham Hotspur Story, Anton Rippon

BRADSHAW, TOM. He signed for Spurs in May 1898 from

Liverpool, where he had been a member of their Second Division winning teams of 1894 and 1896. A fast, direct winger, he was only with Spurs for one season, but in that time played for the United League against the Thames and Medway League, the South against the North and for an England XI against a Scotland XI. In the summer of 1899 he joined Thames Ironworks, but fell ill and died on Christmas Day, aged only 26.

BREARLEY, JOHN. Signed from Everton by John Cameron, Brearley had built quite a reputation as a goalscoring centre-forward. But it was as a half-back that he was to give sterling service to Spurs . He moved to this position when the great Vivian Woodward took up the role of centre-forward and settled in well. A versatile player, he could also fill in at inside-forward when required and finished his Spurs career at outside-left. On the outbreak of World War One, Brearley was working in Germany and interned at the Ruhleben prison camp along with other well-known footballers, including his former manager John Cameron!

BRETTELL, FRANK. Spurs ' first-ever manager, he had been secretary-manager at Bolton Wanderers before joining the club. Originally from Liverpool, he was one of the founder members of Everton. In his playing days, he was a sturdy full-back and assistant secretary of the Goodison Park club, playing in nearly every position for Everton in their early days. When he retired from playing, he joined the *Liverpool Mercury* as a reporter. As Spurs' manager he introduced the club to the Southern League and persuaded many top northern players to join the club. Remaining at Spurs for less than a year he joined Portsmouth when offered a substantial rise.

BRIGGS, STANLEY. One of the most famous names in London amateur football at the end of the last century, Stanley Briggs played an important role in helping to establish Spurs. A tall, commanding half-back he was Spurs' captain and a regular for London and Middlesex. There is no doubt that he would have assisted Spurs for many more years were it not for the club's decision in December 1895 to adopt professionalism. Briggs was totally against this and even refused to attend the meeting at which the proposal was passed. He continued to play for Spurs until the end of the 1897–88 season and then joined Clapton. Had he played professionally, he would probably have played for England although he did play for the FA XI that toured Germany and Bohemia in November 1899.

BROOKE, GARRY. A midfield player with a powerful and accurate long-range shot, he netted twice on his full debut at home to Southampton on Boxing Day 1980. As a teenager, he was a fabulous prospect but hampered by both soccer injuries and those sustained in a car crash, he never really became a first-team regular. In fact, he may well go down in history as the only player to appear as a substitute in three FA Cup final matches. He came on for Ricky Villa when Spurs trailed to Manchester City in 1981 and repeated the feat the following year playing as substitute in both matches against Queen's Park Rangers. Although he recovered from the injuries sustained in a car crash in February 1983 he was never the same player and joined Norwich City for £50,000. Unable to break through at Carrow Road he moved to Groningen of Holland before returning to London with Wimbledon. Not happy with their direct style of play, he signed for Brentford and linked up with former Spurs player Phil Holder. Still unable to establish himself in the Football League, he joined Colchester United on loan and then had a trial with Reading before playing for a number of non-League clubs.

BROOKS, JOHNNY. After arriving from Reading in February 1953 he found it hard to make the step up to the First Division as Arthur Rowe set about major surgery to his beloved 'push and run' title winners. However, by the end of the 1954–55 season he had established a regular place and when Eddie Baily left in January 1956 he assumed the main creative role. A naturally gifted player, he had brilliant dribbling skills and an amazing body swerve. He also possessed a superb touch with either foot and his shooting ability soon caught the eye of the England selectors. He won his first cap against Wales in November 1956 and scored, as he did in his second match. However, his third against Denmark was his last as he did not fit in with Johnny Haynes, England's senior schemer. There was always a worrying lack of consistency with Johnny Brooks and within a month of playing for England, he was dropped by his club. In December 1959 he moved to

Chelsea in a £20,000 part-exchange for Les Allen. Having helped stave off relegation, he didn't stay long at Stamford Bridge and saw out his career in the lower divisions with Brentford and Crystal Palace.

BROWN, BILL. When he signed from Dundee for £16,000 in June 1959, he was already a Scottish international. He went on to win 28 caps which was a record for a Scottish goalkeeper at the time. Tall, lean and agile and a superb shot-stopper, he soon established himself as a worthy successor to Ted Ditchburn. His powers of concentration and calmness were other attributes that helped Spurs achieve the 'double' in 1960–61, a season in which he missed only one game, win the FA Cup in 1961–62 and the European Cup-winners' Cup in 1962–63. On the way to the final of this latter competition he was seen at his best. In the quarter-final first-leg defeat by Slovan Bratislava, he played with a plaster across his nose after taking a heavy knock and defied the Czechs with a series of outstanding saves, limiting their lead to two goals and paving the way for eventual victory. There followed two great semi-final displays against OFK Belgrade before he performed wonders in the final itself as Atletico Madrid peppered his goal for 15 minutes in a constant onslaught. By the mid-1960s injuries and the emergence of Pat Jennings led to his move to Northampton Town, having played his last game for Spurs in a friendly at Dundee in October 1966. He remained with the Cobblers until the end of the season before playing for Toronto Falcons in the 'rebel' American Professional Soccer League.

BROWN, BOB. A solid, dependable full-back, he made his senior debut in a London FA Charity Cup match with Crystal Palace in October 1919 but had to wait until the end of the year for his League debut. He then held his place and played 20 games as Spurs won the Second Division title. Unable to reproduce his earlier form, he was consigned to the reserves although his cause was not helped by a number of injuries. Transfer-listed in April 1925, he received several offers, but refused them all and retired to run a butcher's shop in Southampton!

BROWN, SANDY. Though he was with Spurs for only two seasons, his goalscoring impact was immediate, for it was his goals that were responsible for the club's first-ever FA Cup victory at the end of his initial season. He scored in every round of the competition proper and his total of 15 FA Cup goals that season is still a record. He scored both the goals in the 1901 final and then added the deciding strike in the Final replay. He had joined Spurs from Portsmouth, where one newspaper reporter informed his public that Brown was called 'Sandy' as a common adaptation of Alexander and it had nothing to do with his hair colouring. While with Spurs he was selected for the Ibrox-disaster Scotland v England game of 1902 but at the end of the season he returned to Portsmouth. In the close season of 1903 he moved to Middlesbrough, where he at last won a Scottish cap playing against England in April 1904.

BROTHERS. There have been a number of instances of brothers playing for Tottenham Hotspur. The most famous were the Steel brothers. The youngest of the three was Bobby, a regular scorer and one of the stars of Spurs' early days in the Football League. Danny Steel was a strong-tackling individual who along with Bobby, formed the core of the Spurs team. Alex Steel's only appearance for Spurs was alongside his two brothers in a League game against Bradford City in January 1910. It is the only occasion on which Spurs have fielded three brothers in the same League game.

BUCKINGHAM, VIC. In 16 years at White Hart Lane, he never played in the First Division, a record which may show why this tall, stylish player later sought and achieved success as a coach and manager. After making his debut against Bury in November 1935, he became established at half-back, but like so many of his generation, the best years of his career were lost to the war. Serving in the RAF, he guested for other clubs, even playing for Portsmouth against Spurs and appeared for England in two wartime internationals against Wales. When he resumed his first-team career it was at full-back because Nicholson and Burgess were the Spurs' wing-halves. In 1947–48 he was a Division Two ever-present but early in the 1949–50 season he retired, having spent his entire career with Spurs. He took to coaching the juniors but in June 1951 his talents were recognised by Bradford Park Avenue and he became their manager. In February he took over at West

Bromwich Albion and in his first year they won the FA Cup and finished runners-up in Division One. On leaving the Hawthorns, he coached Ajax of Amsterdam before returning to England to manage Sheffield Wednesday. In January 1965 he joined Fulham but after three years of struggling to avoid relegation he left. He later managed Ethnikos of Greece and Spanish clubs Barcelona and Sevilla.

BULL, WALTER. Signed from Notts County in May 1904, Walter Bull was one of the most highly rated footballers in the game. In his eight years at Meadow Lane he was regarded as something of a utility player, appearing in every outfield position. He had appeared in the first major game staged at White Hart Lane, playing a friendly against Spurs in September 1899. Although Bull never played for England, he did play in four trial matches and was first reserve to the England team on a number of occasions. A member of the committee when the Players' Union was formed in 1907, Bull later went to coach in Buenos Aires having previously visited Argentina with Spurs' touring party in 1909. He returned in July 1912, replacing Herbert Chapman as manager of Northampton Town.

BURGESS, RON. One of football's all-time greats, he arrived at Spurs in May 1936 as a forward and a year later was about to be released when he played for the 'A' team at wing-half as a late

"TURF" CIGARETTES

RONNIE BURGESS
TOTTENHAM H. & WALES
50 FOOTBALLERS No 19

replacement. Spurs changed their minds and offered him a place on the ground staff and an amateur contract at the Northfleet nursery. He gained a first-team place at right-half and within nine months of making his debut he was playing international football for Wales. Throughout the war years he won representative honours for the RAF, FA and his country, turning out for Spurs when service demands permitted, if not guesting for Notts County. After the war he settled into the left-half position and captained Spurs for eight consecutive seasons, leading them to the Second Division championship and the League championship in successive seasons. He was also captain of his country, winning 32 caps between 1946 and 1954 when he missed only two internationals. He was the first Welshman to play for the English Football League and he played for Great Britain against the Rest of Europe in 1947. In May 1954, shortly after making his final appearance for his country, he took the job of player-coach with Swansea Town before graduating to player-manager and then taking over the manager's job full time. Four years later he moved to Watford as manager and there discovered and transferred Pat Jennings to Spurs.

BURKINSHAW, KEITH. A South Yorkshireman, he first worked at Dodworth Colliery transporting tubs of coal from the pit face before joining Liverpool. He only played one game for their first team before he was transferred to Workington. Over the next seven-and-a-half seasons, he made 293 League appearances for the Cumbrian club. In May 1965 he moved to become player-manager at Scunthorpe United, before going to coach in Zambia. After a short time he returned to these shores to become first-team coach at Newcastle United. A year after helping the Magpies to reach Wembley in 1974, he was controversially sacked. He joined Spurs in a similar capacity before becoming manager in July 1976 following Terry McNeill's resignation. He couldn't prevent Spurs dropping into Division Two at the end of his first term in charge, but promotion the following season justified the board's decision to retain faith with the honest Yorkshireman. In 1978 he caught the imagination of the soccer world with the bold acquisition of Argentinians, Ardiles and Villa. He assembled an attractive squad of players, which, though never consistent enough to lift the League championship, won the FA Cup in 1981 and 1982 and the UEFA Cup in 1984. He became unhappy with boardroom politics and announced that when the 1983–84 season ended, he would resign. He moved to the Middle East to manage the Bahrain national team before managing Sporting Lisbon of Portugal. He later managed Gillingham before becoming Ardiles' right-hand man at West Bromwich Albion.

BURROWS, LY. Although born at Ashton-under-Lyne in Lancashire, Burrows' family moved around a lot and he first played football for the Melrose club of Govan near Glasgow. He then played for his school team in Sheffield before moving down to London, where he joined the Woolwich Polytechnic club. It was whilst playing for the latter that he caught the attention of Woolwich Arsenal. One of the great characters of London football at this time, he gained a reputation for being a 'hard man' and accepted an invitation to play for Spurs in 1894. He still turned out in ten Football League games for Woolwich Arsenal but was primarily recognised as a Spurs player. His robust skills certainly helped establish Spurs in the Southern League but in December 1897 Burrows announced that he was moving back to Sheffield for business reasons and joined Sheffield United.

BURTON, OLLIE. Originally a half-back like his brother John, his best service to Spurs came at full-back. He established himself slowly at Spurs, eventually replacing his brother in the half-back line. However, he was a little out of his depth in the middle of the park and in December 1905 he was tried at full-back when Sandy Tait was injured. A strong, muscular player, he made the position his own. He was virtually an ever-present in 1907–08 and the following season, which was the club's first in the Football League. After promotion to the First Division, he found the job harder and dropped out of the team after only five matches.

C

CAMERON, JOHN. There is no doubt that the signing of John Cameron in May 1898 was a major catalyst in the rise of Tottenham Hotspur. Within three years the club had won the Southern League championship and the FA Cup. Born in Ayr, he first won fame with Queen's Park before moving to Everton. He earned his living working in the Liverpool offices of the Cunard shipping line, but this was not popular with his Goodison teammates and so he signed for Spurs . A goalscoring inside-forward, he was also a great dribbler and possessed excellent passing ability. Cameron had a reputation as an articulate person and soon became secretary-manager of Spurs and secretary of the Players and Trainers Union. After the successes of winning the Southern League and FA Cup, Cameron was unable to maintain such high standards, although second place in the Southern League was achieved in 1901–02 and 1903–04. Thereafter he began to take a less active role on the pitch, preferring to concentrate on his administrative and managerial duties. Although the team was not successful, Cameron's popularity was such that no pressure was put on him. The club even brought in Arthur Turner to take over the secretarial duties so that Cameron could focus his attention on team affairs. However, in March 1907 he resigned, giving 'differences with the directorate' as his reason.

CANTRELL, JIMMY. Jimmy Cantrell came to Tottenham from Notts County. In three of his four seasons at Meadow Lane he was top scorer and regarded as one of the best centre-forwards around. On 12 October 1912 he had scored two goals for Notts County against Spurs at White Hart Lane when, after 80 minutes, fog descended and the game was abandoned with County 3–1 ahead. The following Friday he signed for Spurs. Cantrell was a subtle centre-forward rather than the typical battering-ram player of his day. He was an artist who preferred to stroke the ball goalwards rather than blast his shots. He was unlucky never to win international honours but was frequently first reserve, and even when chosen for the Football League side, had to miss out on the honour due to injury. When the First World War broke out, he returned to the Midlands and frequently assisted Notts County, but when the game resumed in 1919, he returned to Spurs. Surprisingly, for he was now 37 years of age, he still had enough skill and speed of thought to play in the Second Division winning team of 1919–20 and scored 18 goals in his 29 appearances. The following season he still led the line as Spurs beat Wolves in the FA Cup final and he played his last game for the club in April 1923 just a few weeks short of 41st birthday – the oldest player to appear for the club in the Football League.

CAPACITY. The total capacity of White Hart Lane in 1995 was 33,147. The breakdown was as follows:
Members' Stand North: 6,932
West Stand: 6,891
East Stand: 10,860
South Stand: 8,464

CAPS. The most capped player in the club's history is Pat Jennings who won 75 caps for Northern Ireland.

CAPS (ENGLAND). The first Spurs player to be capped by England was Fanny Walden when he played against Scotland in 1914. The most capped player is Glenn Hoddle with 44 caps.

CAPS (NORTHERN IRELAND). The first Spurs player to be capped by Northern Ireland was Dick Rowley when he played against Wales in 1931. The most capped player is Pat Jennings.

CAPS (SCOTLAND). The first Spurs player to be capped by Scotland was Sandy Brown when he played against England in 1902, although the match was later declared unofficial following the crowd disaster. The most capped player is Bill Brown with 24 caps.

CAPS (WALES). The first Spurs player to be capped by Wales was John L. Jones when he played against Ireland in 1898. The most capped player is Cliff Jones with 41 caps.

CAPTAINS. Among the many players who have captained the club were John L. Jones who skippered the club to its first FA Cup success in 1901, and Arthur Grimsdell who was captain of Spurs' 1921 FA Cup winning side. Ron Burgess captained Spurs for eight seasons after the Second World War, leading the club to the Second Division championship and the League championship in successive seasons. Danny Blanchflower captained the club to its greatest ever triumph of the League and FA Cup double in 1961 whilst one of Spurs' most loyal players,m Steve Perryman, captained the club to success in the 1981 and 1982 FA Cup finals. Graham Roberts led the side to victory in the 1984 UEFA Cup final whilst, more recently, Gary Mabbutt led the club to its record eighth FA Cup win in 1991.

CENTENARY. Spurs celebrated their centenary in 1981–82. Despite losing their first two home League games, they went close to sweeping all the honours. They reached the semi-finals of the European Cup-winners' Cup before losing to Barcelona and were beaten after extra-time by Liverpool in the Football League Cup final. As the season came to a close, injuries and fatigue took their toll and they finished fourth. The club desperately wanted to mark their 100 years with a trophy – Queen's Park Rangers provided stubborn opposition and it took a Glenn Hoddle penalty to settle the issue after the first game had been drawn to bring the FA Cup to White Hart Lane.

CENTURIES. There are eight instances of individual players who have scored 100 or more League goals for Spurs. Jimmy Greaves is the greatest goalscorer with 220 strikes in his Tottenham career (1961–70). Other centurions are Bobby Smith (176), Cliff Jones

(135), George Hunt (125), Martin Chivers (118), Len Duquemin (114), Les Bennett (104) and Jimmy Dimmock (100). Ted Ditchburn holds the club record for the most consecutive League appearances – 247. Other players to have made over 100 consecutive appearances during their careers are Steve Perryman (189), Pat Jennings (162), Cyril Spiers (122), Tony Marchi (116), Cyril Knowles (114), Billy Minter (108), Steve Perryman (107 in a second spell), Ron Henry (105), Ray Clemence (103), Keith Osgood (102), Danny Blanchflower (102) and Jimmy Dimmock (100).

CHAMPIONSHIPS. Spurs have won the League championship on two occasions. The first of these was in 1950–51 when they finished three points ahead of Manchester United. Things did not look so good after the first game of the season, for Blackpool visited White Hart Lane and won 4–1. During the months of October and November, Spurs were involved in an eight-match winning sequence and successive home matches saw Stoke beaten 6–1, Portsmouth 5–1 and Newcastle 7–0. The club's new fast-flowing brand of football brought the fans back to White Hart Lane and the title in the penultimate game of the season. The second occasion was in 1960–61 when they also won the FA Cup. In the League, the first 11 games were all won and the club's first defeat came in the 17th game – both records. Thirty-one matches were won – another record. Sixteen away matches were won – another record. Sixty-six points were secured, this equalling a record. The championship was won by eight points from Sheffield Wednesday.

CHANNELL, FRED. Associated with the club immediately on leaving school, Fred Channell worked his way through a number of clubs that acted as Spurs' 'nurseries' before making his League debut against Sunderland in October 1933. Replacing the injured Bill Felton, he took to the right-back position so well that the experienced Felton was allowed to leave. Channell was a stylish defender and highly rated by the club. In March 1935 he played for The Rest in the England trial at the Hawthorns and then for an English XI against an Anglo-Scots XI at Highbury two months later. Just as his career was reaching its peak, he was so badly injured in the 3–1 defeat by West Ham on 14 March 1936 that, two months later, at the age of only 26, he was forced to retire.

CHAPLIN, JOHN. Popular with the Spurs fans, John Chaplin made his senior debut for the club against Plymouth Argyle in a Western League fixture in October 1905. Displacing John Watson as first choice right-back in 1906, he went on to make 102 first-team appearances. At the end of the 1907–08 season Spurs wanted to re-sign him but surprisingly he opted to return to Dundee, his home town club. In November 1910 he tried to join Manchester City but Spurs' consent was needed. As they had offered Chaplin the maximum permitted wages in 1908, they had first claim on his services. They did not stand in his way, but after only 17 appearances for the Hyde Road club, injury brought his career to an end.

CHAPMAN, HERBERT. One of the greatest names in football, he joined Spurs in March 1905, an inside-forward with plenty of experience gained throughout the country. After starting as an amateur with his local club, Kiveton Park, Sheffield, he moved to Ashton North End and Stalybridge Rovers before turning professional. He then played for Rochdale, Grimsby Town, Swindon Town, Sheppey United, Worksop and Northampton Town but reverted to amateur status when spending the 1902–03 season with Sheffield United. He then turned back to the professional ranks, joining Notts County, and the following season he again played for Northampton. Spurs paid County a £70 transfer fee, for they still held his registration. Almost an ever-present in his first full season of 1905–06, he was relegated to the reserves the following season before rejoining Northampton. After the First World War he managed Huddersfield Town and led them to the FA Cup in 1922 and the League title in 1924 and 1925. He joined Arsenal and in 1927 took the Gunners to the FA Cup final where they lost to Cardiff City. Three years later he took them back to Wembley again to beat his old club Huddersfield Town. In 1931 Arsenal won the League championship and the FA Cup the following year before winning the League title again in 1933. This great Arsenal side were on their way to the second of three successive titles when, unfortunately, Herbert Chapman died of pneumonia.

CHARITY SHIELD. Tottenham Hotspur have appeared in the Charity Shield on nine occasions:

1920 v West Bromwich Albion (at White Hart Lane) 0–2
1921 v Burnley (at White Hart Lane) 2–0
1951 v Newcastle United (at White Hart Lane) 2–1
1961 v FA XI (at White Hart Lane) 3–2
1962 v Ipswich Town (at Portman Road) 5–1
1967 v Manchester United (at Old Trafford) 3–3
1981 v Aston Villa (at Wembley) 2–2
1982 v Liverpool (at Wembley) 0–1
1991 v Arsenal (at Wembley) 0–0
In the 1967 game, Spurs goalkeeper Pat Jennings scored a goal with a clearance from his own penalty area.

CHELSEA. In 1909–10 the club's fate was not resolved until the last match of the season against neighbours Chelsea. Chelsea had 29 points, Spurs had 30, and when the teams met at White Hart Lane one or other had to go down with bottom club Bolton Wanderers. The unlucky ones were Chelsea with Tottenham scraping home 2–1, courtesy of goals by Minter and Humphreys.

CHIEDOZIE, JOHN. The fleet-footed Nigerian, whose family had left Africa when he was 12 years old, had earned a glowing reputation with Orient before joining Tottenham for £375,000 from Notts County in August 1984. He was a regular Nigerian international when signed and made three further appearances for his country whilst at White Hart Lane. He flourished in the 1984–85 season as Spurs' enterprising 4-2-4 system sustained their title challenge well into April. The next term saw his progress halted by both injuries and the arrival of Chris Waddle and Paul Allen. A nice, easy-going character, he was released in 1988 and had spells with Derby, Notts County and Chesterfield before dropping into non-League football with Banks of Barking and Bashley.

CHIVERS, MARTIN. He joined Spurs from Southampton in January 1968, valued at a record fee of £125,000 in the deal that took Frank Saul (valued at £45,000) to The Dell. He scored on his debut at Sheffield Wednesday and then grabbed both goals in the following match, a third round FA Cup 2–2 draw at Old Trafford. In September of that year he twisted his knee and was sidelined for a year. His recovery was such that in the spring of 1970, with

Martin Chivers

Jimmy Greaves having departed, he was the club's chief goal-get-ter. already the holder of a record number of England Under-23 caps (17) he played 24 times, scoring 13 goals for the full interna-tional team. Having scored both Spurs' goals in the 1971 Football League Cup final victory over Aston Villa, the goals kept coming. Though he could look clumsy and casual, he was deceptive for such a big man and scored some spectacular goals. Against Wolves at Molineux in the first leg of the 1972 UEFA Cup final, he hit home a stunning 25-yarder after beating two men and a soaring header, whilst a 35-yard free-kick of tremendous velocity provid-ed a crucial away goal against Victoria Setubal in March 1973. A player whose long throw-in was a powerful weapon, he finally left Spurs in July 1976 for £80,000 to join Swiss club Servette Geneva. He later had short spells at Norwich and Brighton but was no longer up to the demands of League football.

CLAESEN, NICO. He arrived at White Hart Lane in October 1986, a £600,000 acquisition from Standard Liege. It was with

Standard that he rose to fame, playing an important role in helping Belgium reach the semi-finals of the 1986 World Cup in Mexico. Elusive to mark, he was used at first as a conventional front-runner alongside Clive Allen, but manager Pleat experimented with tactics and Claesen suffered as Allen played in front of a five-man midfield. Whilst he continued to play for his country, he had to be content to settle for the substitute's role, including the 1978 FA Cup final against Coventry. Not surprisingly, he was not satisfied with his reserve role and in August 1988 he joined Antwerp for £550,000.

CLARKE, HARRY. One of the best buys Arthur Rowe ever made for Spurs, Harry Clarke helped Lovells Athletic win the Welsh Cup in 1948, before joining the White Hart Lane club in March 1949. Despite his late entry into the game (he was 26) he maintained an ever-present place for the next two seasons, when Spurs won the Second Division and Football League titles. After missing the start of the 1951–52 season, he came back to continue his impressive performances. He won an England 'B' cap and in April 1954 played for the full international team in a 4–2 win at Hampden Park. He retired from playing during the 1956–57 season, but remained at White Hart Lane as a coach to the younger players.

CLAWLEY, GEORGE. One of the most reliable of goalkeepers, George Clawley made his name at Southampton in the 1890s, helping them to win the Southern League title in 1897 and 1898. He had one season at Stoke before John Cameron signed him for Spurs. A month after making his debut he broke his leg and missed most of the Southern League championship season when he played in all Spurs' matches in their magnificent FA Cup run. He was particularly strong in dealing with corners and crosses and was almost irreplaceable over the next two seasons. Though he played in an international trial match at White Hart Lane in March 1903, major representative honours eluded him. At the end of that season he returned to Southampton and won a Southern League championship medal with them the following year.

CLAY, TOMMY. Idolised by young supporters as one of the finest full-backs of his day, Tommy Clay provided one of the longest and most impressive playing careers in Spurs history. He was a Spurs regular for 12 years after his transfer from Leicester Fosse in January 1914. Hard tackling and an immaculate passer of the ball, he was renowned for his positional play and application of the old offside law. He played for Spurs throughout the First World War and was a reliable penalty-taker for the club. In April 1919 he played in an international trial match but did not win a first cap until March 1920 when he played against Wales at Highbury. He was club captain when Spurs won the Second Division title in 1919–20 but handed over to Arthur Grimsdell so missed the honour of lifting the FA Cup after an immaculate display in the 1921 final. Around this time he won another four caps and represented the Football League and even played one whole match in goal, when both Spurs goalkeepers were injured. Clay kept a clean sheet that day as Spurs beat Sunderland 1–0 at Roker Park. He stayed at White Hart Lane until 1929 when he moved to Northfleet to coach players at Spurs' nursery club.

CLAYTON, EDDIE. An intelligent, ball-playing inside-forward, Eddie Clayton scored twice on his debut in Spurs' 4–3 victory over Everton at Goodison Park. His best season at Tottenham was 1965–66 when he was almost an ever-present, playing in 38 games. With the arrival of Terry Venables from Chelsea, Clayton, a fine young player who never quite made a success of his career, was allowed to leave for Southend United. After two seasons he moved on to Margate and in 1973 played against Spurs in the third round of the FA Cup.

CLEAN SHEET. This is the colloquial expression to describe a goalkeeper's performance when he does not concede a goal. Pat Jennings in 1970–71 had 20 clean sheets from 40 League appearances, plus another five in Cup competitions. The next best performance is by Bill Jacques, who kept 19 clean sheets in 42 appearances in 1919–20.

CLEMENCE, RAY. When he joined Spurs from Liverpool for £300,000 in August 1981, he had won almost every honour in the game. Making his Football League debut for Scunthorpe United, he went on to make 50 senior appearances for the Irons before joining Liverpool for £15,000. After serving a lengthy stint in the Anfield reserves, he took over from Tommy Lawrence as the first choice 'keeper in 1970–71 and missed only six League games in his 11 seasons with the Reds. During that time, Liverpool won the League five times, the European Cup on three occasions, the UEFA Cup twice, the FA Cup once and the League Cup. To this list of club honours he could add 56 England caps, four at Under-23 level and two appearances for the Football League. Signed by Keith Burkinshaw for £300,000 in August 1981 he made his debut at Wembley in the FA Charity Shield. In that opening season he helped Spurs to retain the FA Cup and reach the League Cup final where they lost to his former club. With Spurs he increased his total of England caps to 61 and would have won many more if he had not been competing on the international scene with Peter Shilton. He completed 1,000 first-class games in 1985 and was rewarded for his services to football with the OBE in the 1987 Birthday Honours List. In the 1987–88 season his career was interrupted by injury which kept him out of the team, whereupon he accepted a coaching post with the club, which led to his appointment as assistant to chief coach Doug Livemore in 1992. In January 1994 he became manager of Barnet.

CLEMENTS, BOB. Bob Clements was first associated with the club in its amateur days. In Spurs' first Southern League campaign of 1896–97 he was the top scorer. However, he was one of the early players who suffered from the club's decision to turn professional and though he was retained at the end of that season, the arrival of Bob Stormont meant he could not get in the team.

COATES, RALPH. Making his League debut for Burnley in December 1964 he quickly established a reputation as a promising player and in his time at Turf Moor won eight England Under-23 caps, played four times for the Football League and won two England caps. Joining Spurs for £190,000 in May 1971, his first two games as a Spurs player were for England, his third and fourth caps. He played for Spurs in the UEFA Cup final of 1972 and scored the only goal of the 1973 League Cup final after coming on as a substitute. Though he could play on the wing or in midfield, he never really settled in either spot and this is probably why he never truly completed the spectacular development that the White Hart Lane fans expected. An energetic player with Bobby Charlton-like strands of fair hair covering a receding hair-line, he left White Hart Lane in the summer of 1978 to play for the St George's Club of Sydney but returned after a few months to play for Orient.

COCA-COLA CUP. See Football League Cup.

COLLINS, PETER. A strong, rugged central defender, he cost just £5,500 when he came from Southern League Chelmsford City with a further £4,000 after ten first-team appearances. During his time at White Hart Lane he continually challenged Mike England and Phil Beal for one of the central defensive roles. England's injury in the 1970–71 season gave him a long run and he took the opportunity well, winning a League Cup winners' medal for his pains. The following season saw him return to the reserve ranks, but he continued to distinguish himself whenever called to the first-team colours. Unfortunately, he sustained a seri-ous ankle injury and despite a lengthy battle to try and overcome it, he was forced to retire from League football early. He later had spells as player-boss at Folkestone, manager of Malden Town and helped with the coaching at Southend and Chelmsford City.

COLLINS, TOM. He came to prominence playing with Hearts, for the Scottish League against the Football League in February 1909 and for Scotland against Wales the following month. Joining Spurs in November 1910 he soon became established as the club's first choice right-back. Fast and strong in the tackle, he played for the Anglo-Scots against the Home Scots in both 1911 and 1912 and was unlucky not to win more international caps. During the First World War he sustained serious injuries in the trenches and lost both an arm and a leg. Further football was obviously impos-sible and in March 1915 his contract was cancelled by mutual con-sent.

COLOURS. During their early years, Spurs played in navy-blue with a scarlet shield bearing the letter 'H'. After watching Blackburn Rovers defeat Queen's Park in the FA Cup final, the club changed their colours to the Blackburn style of blue-and-white halves for the 1885–86 season. A decision was taken in

1892–93 to change the club colours yet again, this time to red shirts and blue shorts. These colours were retained until Spurs joined the Southern League in 1896–97 when they were changed to chocolate and gold. Just before the start of the 1899–1900 season Spurs changed their colours to the present-day scheme as a tribute to Preston North End, the most successful team of the time.

CONN, ALFIE. Bill Nicholson's last signing for Spurs . Alfie Conn, the £140,000 purchase from Rangers, was hailed as a magical talent. A member of Rangers' winning teams in the 1971 Scottish League Cup final and 1973 Scottish Cup final, he also helped them win the European Cup-winners' Cup in 1972. He made only one appearance for Spurs under Nicholson's management before the arrival of Terry Neill. One League appearance as a substitute was followed by his full debut at Newcastle United on 11 January 1975. He celebrated in great style with a hat-trick in Spurs' best victory of the season. A natural showman, he was always prepared to take a man on and beat him with pure skill. He rapidly gained cult hero status, but was not helped by a series of injuries that were the direct consequence of his style of play. He had a very chequered career at White Hart Lane for, after winning two full international caps in May 1975, he found himself languishing in the reserves. In March 1977 he joined Celtic, playing in their 1977 Scottish Cup final success and helping them lift the Scottish League title in both 1977 and 1979.

CONSECUTIVE HOME GAMES. Spurs played an extraordinary, intense sequence of six home games in succession in just 21 days (14 February–7 March 1987). They won four – Southampton (2–0), Leicester City (5–0), Queen's Park Rangers (1–0) in the League and Newcastle United (1–0) in the FA Cup but lost both Football League Cup semi-final encounters with Arsenal 2–1.

CONSECUTIVE SCORING – LONGEST SEQUENCE. Jimmy Greaves holds the club record for consecutive scoring when he was on target in nine consecutive League games. His first came in the 2–2 draw with Bolton Wanderers at White Hart Lane on 24 February 1962 and ended with the third goal in Spurs' 4–1 home win over Blackburn Rovers on 20 April.

COOK, BILLY. He made his mark with Bishop Auckland, helping them win the FA Amateur Cup in 1921 and 1922. After a short spell with Rotherham United, he signed for Herbert Chapman's Huddersfield Town and helped them to three successive Football League titles between 1924 and 1927 before joining Aston Villa. Although he was 34 when he signed for Spurs, this accomplished player gave the club two years' sterling service.

COPELAND, DAVID. One of the many Scots recruited by the club, David Copeland played a considerable part in Spurs' run of success at the turn of the century as they won the Southern League championship and the FA Cup. He had played for Ayr Parkhouse, Walsall and Bedminster, mainly as a winger or centre-forward, but at Spurs he was soon switched to inside-forward, where he achieved most of his success. He was joint top scorer with Tom Pratt as Spurs won their only Southern League title and along with Cameron was responsible for many of the goals scored by Sandy Brown. He also had a marvellous understanding with his winger, John Kirwan, and had they been of the same nationality there is little doubt Copeland would have won international honours. As it was, the nearest he got was an appearance for the Anglo-Scots against the Home Scots in the 1903 international trial. He stayed with Spurs until May 1905 when both he and Kirwan moved to Chelsea. A broken leg early in the 1906–07 season virtually ended his career although he did attempt a comeback with Glossop, but was only able to play two games for them. A few seasons before the First World War he turned out for Walsall in the Birmingham League although his goalscoring capabilities had not surprisingly waned.

COTTRELL, FRANK. One of the longest-serving players from the club's early days, he made his debut in the 1883–84 season against Brownlow Rovers, the initial match for which a full Spurs line-up is recorded. He appeared regularly right up until the 1892–93 campaign, but after that he made only one appearance in each of the next three seasons. His association with the club came to an end when they turned professional, for he was not up to the standards required.

COX, FREDDIE. Robbed of most of his best playing years by the

Second World War, during which he was awarded the Distinguished Flying Cross, Freddie Cox was Spurs' first-choice winger in the early post-war years. With the emergence of Sonny Walters, he was allowed to move to Arsenal for £12,000. Ironically, it was at Highbury that Freddie Cox enjoyed his greatest successes and he always relished return visits to White Hart Lane. In July 1953 he left the Gunners to join former Spurs colleague Vic Buckingham at West Bromwich Albion initially as player-coach but later assistant manager. He later became manager at Bournemouth and was in charge when the Cherries knocked Spurs out of the FA Cup in February 1957.

CRICKETERS. The only Tottenham players who were cricketers of real note were Bill Edrich, Fanny Walden and George Leach. Between 1934 and 1958, Bill Edrich scored 36,965 runs with 86 centuries. He was also a fine bowler, taking 479 wickets, and a superb slip fielder. In the summer of 1947, he and his brilliant batting partner, Denis Compton, were record-breaking idols who drew large crowds everywhere they played. Edrich hit a remarkable 3,539 runs at an average of 80.43. Fanny Walden played for Northamptonshire. A useful batsman, he scored 7,462 runs and took 114 wickets in 258 matches for the county. He later became a first-class umpire, reaching Test match standard. George Leach played 225 games for Sussex between 1903 and 1914, scoring 5,788 runs and taking 413 wickets.

CROOKS, GARTH. Born in the Potteries of Jamaican parents, he helped his hometown club, Stoke City, into the First Division in 1978–79 and won his first England Under-21 cap in November 1979 when he scored a hat-trick against Bulgaria. Signed in July 1980 for £600,000 he scored in his first three games and formed a partnership with Steve Archibald which was to take Spurs to two consecutive FA Cup finals. In fact, he played in 17 FA Cup ties for the club before experiencing defeat. He scored several important goals in those ties including the two which killed off Wolves in the 1981 semi-final, the equaliser against Manchester City in the final and the winner against Arsenal the following year. Loss of form in the middle of the 1982–83 season saw him lose his place and go on loan to Manchester United. He was given little opportunity at Old Trafford and returned understandably frustrated. In August

1985 he was transferred to West Bromwich Albion for £100,000 but then left the West Midlands side for Charlton Athletic. Despite injury problems he kept them in the First Division until injury finally led to his retirement in November 1990. This also forced him to resign as chairman of the Professional Footballers' Association for whom he had rendered outstanding service.

CROWD TROUBLE. However unwelcome, crowd disturbances are far from a modern phenomenon at major football matches. Behaviour at White Hart Lane has usually been of a high standard and though Spurs' supporters are well renowned for voicing their opinions at suspect referees, the occasions when their demonstrations boil over beyond the verbal are very rare indeed. However, one such occasion did take place on 21 February 1898 when spectators invaded the pitch and assaulted three of the Luton team! Also, two Spurs players, Andy Duncan and Alf Hawley, both walked off the pitch in their careers at Tottenham, unable to take any more of the continual abuse directed at them by the Spurs crowd. On the club's tour to the Argentine in 1908, a troop of cavalry took to the pitch to beat back spectators with the flats of their swords. Apparently the gates had been broken down and the promoters wanted to drive the spectators out so that they would have to pay to get back in!

CUPS. In its history the club has won 15 major trophies. they are: 2 League titles; 8 FA Cups; 2 Football League Cups; 2 UEFA Cups and 1 European Cup-winners' Cup.

D

DAINES, BARRY. Showing considerable patience before establishing himself as Pat Jennings' successor, he made his League debut in November 1971, but in his first five seasons made only 13 senior appearances because of the consistent brilliance of the big Irishman. In the 1976–77 relegation season, Jennings was injured and Daines gained an extended run in the first team. Keith Burkinshaw had so much confidence in him that he sold Jennings to Arsenal in August 1977. Ever-present in the promotion season that followed, Daines was a competent all-rounder, a player who simply got on with his job. However, he did appear to lack self-belief and when Spurs began to struggle in the First Division he came under increasing pressure from Milija Aleksic and Mark Kendall. After playing in the early rounds he missed out on the 1981 FA Cup final and when Ray Clemence arrived later that year, he moved to Hong Kong, before serving Mansfield.

DARNELL, JABEZ. Jabez Darnell gave Spurs over 40 years' loyal service, 15 of them as a player. Although he made his debut against Queen's Park Rangers in 1905, Spurs had a number of wing-halves on their books and so the tough-tackling Darnell had to be content with a place in the reserves for his first couple of seasons. Eventually replacing Ted Hughes, he missed only one game in Spurs' first Football League season of 1908–09. He held down a regular place for the next three seasons before returning to the reserves. Though he was well past his best, he continued to help the club during the war years and only retired in 1919–20 when normal football resumed. He then took up the position of the club's assistant trainer until he retired in 1946.

DAVIES, WILLIAM. When Spurs signed Willie Davies from Notts County in February 1930 he was a Welsh international with 17 caps to his credit. Beginning his career with Swansea, he played in all the forward positions before settling at outside-right. Moving to Cardiff City he played in the 1925 FA Cup final against Sheffield United before joining Notts County. On his arrival at White Hart Lane he filled what had been a problem position for the club and went on to miss only four of the next 105 League and Cup games. When Spurs won promotion in 1932–33 Davies only played in 15 games and at the end of the season he returned to Swansea, where he played for a further three seasons.

DAY, ALF. Alf Day made his international debut for Wales before he had played even one match in the Football League. Arthur Turner, the Spurs secretary, was contacted by the Welsh secretary-manager Ted Robbins, who was desperately searching for players for his injury-ravaged side. Although Day performed well enough, it was his only cap. The development he showed in Spurs ' reserve side did not fully materialise and after only 13 League appearances he was given a free transfer and moved to Millwall.

DEATH. On 21 July 1964, while practising alone at Crews Hill golf course, Enfield, John White was caught in a thunderstorm and sheltered under an oak tree. Lightning struck and, at 27, John White, who was at the peak of his career, was dead.

DEBUTS. Colin Lee grabbed the headlines on his debut, following his transfer from Torquay United. He scored four goals as Bristol Rovers were crushed 9–0 in October 1977. The greatest goalscorer in Spurs' history, Jimmy Greaves, scored a hat-trick in the club's 5–2 home win over Blackpool. Jimmy Brain made a remarkable debut for Arsenal against Spurs in October 1924. Later to join Tottenham, he scored the only goal of the game, although it was not one he knew a great deal about. He was struck by a fierce shot from Jock Rutherford which deflected into the Spurs net and left poor Brain unconscious!

DECORATIONS. The tradition of decorating the handles of the FA Cup with ribbons in the colours of the winning team was started by Tottenham Hotspur who first decorated it during their celebration dinner after winning the trophy as a non-League team in 1901.

DEFEATS – FEWEST. During the 1919–20 season, Spurs went through the 42-match programme and only suffered four defeats as they won the Second Division championship.

DEFEATS – MOST. Spurs' total of 22 defeats during the 1934–35 season is the worst in the club's history. Not surprisingly, they finished bottom of the First Division and were relegated.

DEFEATS – WORST. Spurs' record defeat was when Derby County beat them 8–2 at the Baseball Ground on 16 October 1976. At the end of that season Spurs finished bottom of the First Division and were relegated. The club have had seven goals put past them on six occasions, the last being at Anfield on 2 September 1978 when Liverpool won 7–0. Spurs' worst home defeat is 6–0, a scoreline inflicted twice by Sunderland (1914–15) and Arsenal (1934–35).

DEFENSIVE RECORDS. Spurs' best defensive record was established in 1919–20 and helped the club win the Second Division championship. They conceded just 32 goals in that campaign and were beaten in only four matches. The club also conceded only 32 goals in 1908–09, their opening season in the Football League, but that was from 38 matches. Spurs' worst defensive record was in 1958–59 when they let in 95 goals to finish 18th in Division One.

DERBIES. The rivalry between Tottenham Hotspur and Arsenal has become an established part of the Football League scene. Arsenal, founded in 1886 as Royal Arsenal, became Woolwich Arsenal in 1891 and Arsenal from 1914. In the derby games, the biggest win is 10–1 by Royal Arsenal at Plumstead on 21

September 1889 in a friendly; the biggest win in a first-class game was Arsenal's 6–1 victory at White Hart Lane in the First Division on 6 March 1935. Arsenal also won 5–1 at Highbury that season. Spurs' biggest win in a first-class match is 5–0, a scoreline in two Football League matches both played at White Hart Lane – on Christmas Day 1911 and 4 April 1983. They also achieved the same score in a London League game on 4 November 1901. Remarkably, between February 1958 and October 1963 the clubs played out three 4–4 draws! The two clubs have met in the FA Cup on three occasions with Spurs winning two and losing one. In the Football League Cup, the clubs have met on seven occasions with Spurs winning two and drawing one of the matches. On 19 August 1992 the two clubs met in the FA Charity Shield at Wembley and played out a goalless draw.

DICK, ALISTAIR. An out-and-out winger, Ally Dick was a Scottish Youth international when he joined Spurs as an apprentice in July 1981. By the time he signed professional forms in May 1982 he had already made his Football League debut. Playing against Manchester City on 20 February 1982 he became the youngest player to appear for Spurs in the Football League, aged 16 years and 301 days. After some promising performances in 1983–84 when he picked up a UEFA Cup winners' medal as a substitute for Gary Mabbutt in the second leg against Anderlecht, he faded from contention. In the summer of 1986 he was given a free transfer and joined Ajax of Amsterdam. He never made the grade in Holland and after unsuccessful attempts to break through with Wimbledon and Brighton, he was lost to the game.

DIMMOCK, JIMMY. Writing his name permanently in Spurs' history when he scored the winning goal against Wolves in the 1921 FA Cup final, at Stamford Bridge, Jimmy Dimmock was a very special talent and one of the greatest wingers ever on Tottenham's books. He played a little as an amateur with Clapton Orient during the First World War and joined Spurs in 1919 from

Edmonton Ramblers. He proved a magnificent asset, a well-built outside-left whose clever trickery with the ball earned him immense popularity with the White Hart Lane crowd. He also had a tremendous shot in both feet and yet early in his career it was surprising that he did not get more goals, but he corrected this in the mid-1920s when he became a much more prolific goalscorer. It was also a mystery that he did not win more than the three international caps his talents deserved. Towards the end of his Spurs career he began to put on weight, although he lost none of his artistry. In April 1931 Spurs decided not to retain his services and he was allowed to join Thames, but at the end of the 1931–32 season they folded and he joined Clapton Orient.

DISMISSALS. Neil Ruddock holds the unenviable record of being the first Tottenham player to be dismissed in a Premier League match when Spurs played Crystal Palace on 22 August 1992. When Jimmy Greaves was sent off in a European Cup-winners' Cup semi-final against OFK Belgrade on 24 April 1963 he was the first Spurs player to be sent off since Cecil Poynton 35 years earlier. Alan Mullery was the first England player to be sent off in a full international when he was dismissed in a European Championship match against Yugoslavia on 5 June 1968.

DITCHBURN, TED. The son of a professional boxer, he arrived at Tottenham via the Northfleet nursery club in 1939. His debut was in the Football League South in May 1940 but National Service meant he was only able to play occasionally for Spurs. However, the war did allow him to get an early taste of representative football with the Royal Air Force and FA XIs as well as two England wartime internationals. Losing his early prime to the war, he missed just two League games in the seven post-war seasons – including an unbroken sequence of 247 outings between April 1948 and March 1954. He was ever-present in the Second Division championship team of 1949–50 and the First Division winning team the following season. Ditchburn was a magnificent catcher of crosses, breathtakingly agile on his line and with Alf Ramsey pioneered and perfected the short throw-out, which was so important to Spurs' 'push and run' style of the early 1950s. Unfortunate to play in an era when England were well served by top-class 'keepers, Frank Swift and Bert Williams, he deserved

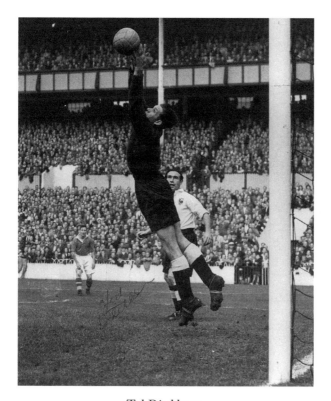

Ted Ditchburn

more than his six England caps which were spread over eight years. In the mid-'50s he lost his place for shot spells to Ron Reynolds but fought his way back. His top-flight days ended with a broken finger at Chelsea in August 1958 and eight months later, by now the only survivor from the 1951 championship team, he became player-manager of non-League Romford. One of the most beloved figures in the history of the club, it is quite remarkable that, when it is taken into account that he lost seven years of his career to the Second World War, only Pat Jennings and Steve Perryman have played more games for Spurs.

DIX, RONNIE. He made his name with Bristol Rovers where he became the youngest player at 15 years 180 days to score a goal in the Football League before moving to Blackburn Rovers, when a proposed transfer to Everton fell through. He only stayed a year at Blackburn before joining Aston Villa. His best years came when he signed for Derby County in February 1937. He played for the

The team which clinched the League and FA Cup double

Football League against the Scottish League and won an England cap, scoring a goal in a 4–0 win over Norway. Spurs signed him in June 1939 but because of the war his White Hart Lane career never got off the ground. During the war he guested for Blackpool and helped them win the Football League North Cup in 1943.

DOUBLE. In 1961 Spurs became the first club this century to clinch the coveted League and FA Cup double, making them the greatest team in English football history.

DRAWS. Spurs played their greatest number of drawn League matches in a single season in 1968–69 when 17 of their matches ended all-square, and their fewest in 1960–61 when only four of their matches were drawn. The club's highest scoring draw is 5–5, a scoreline in three games – v Leicester Fosse (away 1913–14), v Huddersfield Town (home 1925–26) and v Aston Villa (home 1965–66).

DUNCAN, ANDREW. He signed for Spurs in March 1935 after helping Hull City win the Third Division (North) in 1933. A constructive inside-forward, he had the knack of scoring regularly, though he was susceptible to injury. His days at White Hart Lane seemed numbered in 1939 with the arrival of Ronnie Dix, but the intervention of the war allowed an extension to his Spurs career. However, in the opening game of the 1942–43 season against Crystal Palace he said he could not tolerate any more of the crowd's barracking and just walked off the pitch! Although he remained on the club's books, he never wore a Spurs shirt again and guested for Chelmsford City until completing his transfer to them after the war.

DUNCAN, JOHN. Terry Neill's first signing as Tottenham manager, John Duncan's 12 goals in his first season made him top scorer and effectively kept the club in the First Division. An unorthodox and rather awkward centre-forward, his notable average of a goal every other game whilst at White Hart Lane is bettered by only a few select Spurs strikers. He topped the scoring chart again in 1975–76 but a serious back injury saw him miss most of the following campaign when his goals may well have saved the club from relegation. He returned in 1977–78 as Spurs returned to Division One at the first attempt. As manager Keith Burkinshaw planned radical team changes he moved to Derby County for £150,000 in September 1978, later doing well as one of football's more articulate managers.

DUNMORE, DAVE. A dashing centre-forward, his early career at White Hart Lane was restricted by National Service though he did replace Len Duquemin for the local derby at Highbury in February 1954. Showing great promise he was given an extended run to the end of the season. He started the following campaign brightly, netting a hat-trick against Wolves in the second game and kept his place until 'The Duke' returned early in 1955. He then became reserve behind Bobby Smith and so in March 1960 moved to West Ham United. He only spent 12 months with the Hammers, scoring 16 goals in 36 appearances before joining Leyton Orient. He enjoyed his most successful spell with the Os as he top-scored during their promotion to the First Division in 1961–62.

DUQUEMIN, LEN. One of the few Channel Islanders to make his name in the Football League, 'The Duke' was a workmanlike centre-forward who scored many vital goals for Spurs. He had an insatiable appetite for work and was ideally suited to Arthur Rowe's 'push and run' team. He scored the only goal of the game against Sheffield Wednesday which sealed the 1951 League championship and in two FA Cup semi-finals against Blackpool in 1948 and 1953. The arrival of Dave Dunmore in February 1954 put his place in jeopardy, but he fought back and also saw off the challenge from Alfie Stokes. He eventually had to concede the number nine shirt to Bobby Smith and in 1958–59 moved on to Bedford Town.

DURIE, GORDON. After attracting scouts from south of the border, he signed for Chelsea in April 1986 and soon settled to English football, forming a goalscoring partnership with Kerry Dixon. Although dogged by injuries, he still managed to score over 50 League goals for Chelsea, including five in a 7–0 win at Walsall in 1988–89. After winning Under-21 honours, he made his full international debut as a substitute for Scotland in a European Championship qualifying round in Bulgaria. On the eve of the 1991–92 season he was transferred to Spurs for £2.2 million – at the time the club's most expensive acquisition. Remaining relatively injury free in his first season, he played in 31 League games, but unfortunately his goalscoring touch deserted him. After going 17 League games without a goal, he ended his 'drought' with a hat-trick against Coventry City. In his second term he began to form a good partnership with Teddy Sheringham, but then came disaster: talk of a transfer to Glasgow Rangers and an FA enquiry over an alleged 'feigning' injury incident during the home game against Coventry City combined to produce an understandably debilitating effect. Banned for three matches by the FA for trying to get a fellow professional into trouble, a court of appeal eventually overruled the judgement. In November 1993, after months of rumour, he joined Glasgow Rangers for £1.2 million.

DYSON, TERRY. The son of a well-known jockey, 'Ginger' Dyson, he signed for Spurs whilst doing his National Service. An out-and-out winger, his early years at White Hart Lane were spent as understudy to Terry Medwin and George Robb. In fact, he remained very much a reserve in status until the tail-end of the 1959–60 season when he won a place on merit. He was almost an ever-present in the famous 'double' winning team of 1960–61 when he headed the crucial second goal of the FA Cup final against Leicester City. Standing just 5 ft 3 in, he loved every minute of his football and Spurs fans in return loved both his trickery and wholehearted enthusiasm for the game. He started the 1961–62 season in confident style, scoring five goals in three August days, including a hat-trick at home to Arsenal, but Medwin fought back to win his place back from the little Yorkshireman. Determined not to give up, Dyson returned to contribute some glorious moments in the European games of the early 1960s. He scored the winner in Belgrade in the first leg of the 1963 European Cup-winners' Cup semi-final and followed that with two goals (from long-range positions) as Spurs destroyed Atletico Madrid 5–1. After completing two more seasons in the first team he moved to Fulham before going on to Colchester United.

E

EDINBURGH, JUSTIN. Discovered by Southend United, he signed for Spurs for £150,000 in the summer of 1990 after having been on loan for three months at the beginning of the year. After competing with Pat van den Hauwe and Mitchell Thomas for a full-back spot, his year was made complete when, after being selected for Spurs' FA Cup final team against Nottingham Forest, he received a winners' medal following a 2–1 victory. Going on to form a very successful full-back pairing with another ex-Southend United player, Dean Austin, Justin Edinburgh is now a regular member of the Tottenham team.

EDRICH, BILL. Better known as an outstanding Middlesex and England cricketer, Bill Edrich was an outside-left with great pace and an accurate cross. Hailing from Norfolk, he had been an amateur on Norwich City's books but after moving to London to qualify for Middlesex he was persuaded to join Spurs. Within 12 months he had signed professional forms and made his League debut in November 1935. He looked set for a highly promising football career, but cricket was his first love and in 1947 he and Denis Compton (Arsenal and England) were record-breaking idols who drew great crowds wherever they played. It was also the year up to which Spurs held his League registration, such was the high regard in which the club held his footballing talents.

EGGETT, JOHN. A goalkeeper with Doncaster Rovers, John Eggett spent half a season with Woolwich Arsenal without making a League appearance before joining West Ham. Making his debut for Spurs in October 1904, he was virtually immovable for the next two seasons, playing in 119 games. He started the 1906–07 season in similar style but then an injury allowed Matt Reilly to take over the number one position. Unable to get back, he was released and immediately joined the newly professional Croydon Common.

EIRE. The first Spurs player to be capped by the Republic of Ireland was Johnny Gavin when he played against Holland in 1955. The most capped player in Tottenham's history is Chris Hughton who won 52 caps playing for his country.

ELKES, JACK. Jack Elkes had a dream start to his career with Southampton, scoring two goals on his debut. However, a broken collarbone in his next game forced him to miss the rest of the season. He recovered to play the following campaign and after impressing, signed for Spurs in May 1923 for £1,000. A tall, clever footballer, he was unlucky not to win international honours, though he did represent the Football League on three occasions. A member of the FA touring party to Australia in 1925, he also played for the Professionals against the Amateurs in the FA Charity Shield fixture. Though he was best known as an inside-forward and scored 51 goals for Spurs in 201 League and Cup appearances, he was equally at home at centre-half. Not retained at the end of the 1928–29 season, he joined Middlesbrough before ending his career with Watford in 1934.

ELLIOTT, JIMMY. Signed as a centre-forward from Peterborough, he made only 13 Football League appearances for Spurs in his nine years with the club. Moving to half-back he became a regular during the First World War, also playing at full-back or centre-forward. After the war, he made just one League appearance before joining Brentford. After four years he left Griffin Park to travel the world as a coach and manager.

ENGLAND. The first Tottenham player to be capped by England was Fanny Walden who played for England against Scotland on 4

Mike England

April 1914. England lost 3–1. The Tottenham player to win the most England caps is Glenn Hoddle, who made 44 appearances for his country while a Tottenham player. In April 1987, five Tottenham players lined up for England against Turkey in a European Championship qualifier at Izmir. They were Glenn Hoddle, Gary Mabbutt, Steve Hodge, Clive Allen and Chris Waddle. Gary Lineker then with Barcelona also played.

ENGLAND, MIKE. A member of Blackburn Rovers' FA Youth cup winning side of 1959, he went on to become possibly the finest centre-half of his generation. His height made him dominant in the air, whilst on the ground his speed and strength made him the most daunting of defenders for the quickest of opposition forwards. He was equally at home as an attacking wing-half or at centre-forward, where he played very successfully for Rovers. A stubborn and fiercely ambitious player, he threatened to quit the game when Rovers initially refused to allow him to try his luck with a bigger club. After holding out for several months in a one-man rebellion, he signed a one-year contract with Blackburn.

When Rovers were relegated in 1965–66, it became obvious that they would now have to sell their most valuable asset and so England went to White Hart Lane. The fee of £95,000 was a Football League record sum for a defender at the time. Bill Nicholson said: 'I signed him because he likes heading the ball and that's the major part of the job for a player in that position.' England was a key element in the rebuilding of the Tottenham side following the break-up of the legendary double team. His influence was immediate, as Spurs won the FA Cup in 1967, the League Cup in 1971, the UEFA Cup in 1972 and the League Cup again in 1973. Already a regular on the international scene in his days at Ewood, he went on to win 44 caps for Wales as well as 11 Under-23 caps. In March 1975, disheartened by Tottenham's abrupt decline, he decided to retire. However, he re-emerged the following August to play 40 games for Cardiff City, helping them to win promotion from Division Three. He then spent four summers playing for Seattle and appeared for Team America in the 1976 Bi-centennial Tournament with England, Brazil and Italy. He later returned to these shores to become the Welsh national team manager and in 1984 he was awarded the MBE for his services to Welsh soccer.

ERENTZ, HARRY. A Scot of Danish extraction, Harry Erentz was a hard-tackling full-back who made his reputation with Dundee and spent a year with Oldham Athletic before joining Newton Heath. Signed from the Manchester club in May 1898, he immediately became a great favourite with the Spurs fans. Nicknamed 'Tiger', for the ferocity of his tackling, he played a majority of games in Spurs' Southern League championship season of 1899–90 and all the matches in the following season's successful FA Cup run. He stayed with Spurs until the end of the 1903–04 season when he joined Swindon Town.

EUROPEAN CUP. Spurs have participated in Europe's premier competition on only one occasion and that was in 1961–62 following their magnificent 'double' achievement the previous season. In fact, it was the club's first venture into European competition. Their first game was away to Polish champions Gornik Zabrze, and after 30 minutes Spurs found themselves 4–0 down. Two late goals gave them hope for the second leg, which they duly won 8–1! They went on to beat Feyenoord (Holland) and Dukla Prague (Czechoslovakia) before they met the European Cup holders Benfica in the semi-final. Spurs went down 3–1 in Lisbon, though they did have two perfectly good-looking goals disallowed by debatable offside decisions. In the second leg Benfica soon went a goal up and though Greaves seemed to have equalised, the goal was disallowed for offside. A penalty by Blanchflower and a Bobby Smith goal gave Spurs the win, but despite hitting the woodwork three times in the last 40 minutes, Spurs lost 4–3 on aggregate.

EUROPEAN CUP-WINNERS' CUP. The club won this trophy in 1962–63 at the first time of trying. Glasgow Rangers provided the opposition in the first round but they were soundly beaten 8–4 on aggregate. Slovan Bratislava and OFK Belgrade were also defeated as Spurs met Atletico Madrid in the final at Rotterdam. Though the scoreline was 5–1 in Spurs' favour it was quite flattering, for the Spaniards made the men from White Hart Lane fight all the way. Terry Dyson and Jimmy Greaves scored two apiece and John White one, as Spurs became the first British club to win a major European trophy. Defending the trophy the following season, they went down 4–3 on aggregate to Manchester United, this after they had won the first leg 2–0 at White Hart Lane. Their next appearance in this competition was in 1967–68 when they lost on the away-goals rule to Olympique Lyonnais of France. In 1981–82, the club's centenary, they reached the semi-final only to lose to Barcelona. The club's interest in the following season's competition ended as early as the second round as they went down 5–2 on aggregate to Bayern Munich. The last occasion Spurs were involved in this competition was in 1991–92 and though they reached the third round, they were unable to penetrate a defence-minded Feyenoord and went out 1–0 on aggregate.

EVANS, RAY. An England Youth international, Ray Evans was a strong, positive full-back with a superb long-range shot, though his defensive qualities never quite matched his attacking attributes. He could attack on the overlap at great speed and release any number of crosses to the waiting Chivers and Gilzean. He was most unfortunate not to win any major honours in his time at

White Hart Lane, always seeming to lose out to the more experienced Joe Kinnear when the big games came round. There seemed to be no place for him at Spurs and when Millwall offered £35,000 for his services, he accepted the move. He spent two years at The Den before playing with Fulham and Stoke City.

EVANS, TOMMY. Tommy Evans did not sign as a professional for Spurs until the summer of 1931 but had already made his Football League debut against Southampton on Boxing Day 1929, as the club suffered some desperate injury problems. It was only in 1933–34, when the club finished third in the First Division, and 1934–35, when they finished bottom, that Evans had an extended run in the team.

EVANS, WILLIE. One of the stars of Tottenham's team of the 1930s, Welsh international Willie Evans was a regular scorer and created many goals for George Hunt and Taffy O'Callaghan. In his second season he was an ever-present and missed very few matches right up until injury ended his career. Incredibly fast, his international career began with a first appearance against Northern Ireland in December 1932, but sadly, with just six caps to his name, Evans suffered a serious knee injury. It was sustained in a match at Villa Park in November 1936 on his 24th birthday. A cartilage operation followed, but when a second operation was necessary, Spurs decided not to

WILLS'S CIGARETTES

W. EVANS (TOTTENHAM HOTSPUR)

retain his services. Fulham decided he was worth the gamble, but it was not a success and in May 1938 he was forced to retire without a single game for the Cottagers' League team.

EVER-PRESENTS. There have been 48 Tottenham players who have been ever-present throughout a Football League season. The greatest number of ever-present seasons by a Spurs player is eight by Steve Perryman. Next in line is Ted Ditchburn with five.

F

FA CUP. Spurs first participated in the FA Cup in October 1894, making their debut in a first-round qualifying match against West Herts and winning 3–2. Since then they have gone on to win the trophy on eight occasions. Their first appearance in a final was in 1901 when they beat Sheffield United 3–1 at Burnden Park after the first match had been drawn 2–2.

FA CUP FINALS. Spurs have appeared in nine FA Cup finals, winning the trophy on eight occasions, including three that went to a replay.
1901 Sheffield United (Crystal Palace) 2–2
1901 Sheffield United (Burnden Park) 3–1
1921 Wolverhampton Wanderers (Stamford Bridge) 1–0
1961 Leicester City (Wembley) 2–0
1962 Burnley (Wembley) 3–1
1967 Chelsea (Wembley) 2–1
1981 Manchester City (Wembley) 1–1
1981 Manchester City (Wembley) 3–1
1982 Queen's Park Rangers (Wembley) 1-1
1982 Queen's Park Rangers (Wembley) 1–0
1987 Coventry City (Wembley) 2–3
1991 Nottingham Forest (Wembley) 2–1

FA CUP SEMI-FINALS. Spurs have participated in 15 FA Cup semi-finals up to the end of the 1995–96 season.

FAIRCLOUGH, CHRIS. After making his Football League debut for Nottingham Forest on 4 September 1982 at Anfield, he went on to play in over 100 games for Forest despite missing the entire 1985–86 season through injury. With Brian Clough slow to offer Fairclough a new contract, David Pleat was quick to move and the reliable centre-half arrived at White Hart Lane with a £387,500 fee set by the transfer tribunal. An ever-present through Tottenham's troubled 1987–88 campaign, he was injured at Blackburn in November of the following season. Unable to recover his first-team place from Guy Butters, he joined Leeds United on loan in March 1989, a £500,000 cheque later making the move permanent. In 1989–90 he rediscovered his form and was outstanding as his new team lifted the First Division title in 1992. After making 75 Premier League appearances for the Elland Road side he joined Bolton Wanderers for £500,000.

FAIR PLAY. The club can boast an honourable record for fair play, having gone from 1928 all the way to 1965 without a single player being sent off in the Football League. Frank Saul ended this unequalled run when he was dismissed against Burnley at Turf Moor on 4 December 1965.

FALCO, MARK. Despite scoring on his League debut against Bolton Wanderers, he found it difficult to make a permanent breakthrough, even more so when big money signings Steve Archibald and Garth Crooks joined the club. In August 1981 he scored two goals in the FA Charity Shield match against Aston Villa, this signalling the start of a five-week purple patch. But then injury intervened and it wasn't until the 1983–84 season that he won a regular place. He won a UEFA Cup medal in 1984 and stayed another two seasons before moving to Watford for a bargain £350,000. His stay at Vicarage Road was brief before he joined the growing band of expensive English buys at Glasgow Rangers. After five goals in 14 games for the Ibrox outfit he returned to London with Queen's Park Rangers and later Millwall where injury cut short his playing career.

FATHER AND SON. Spurs have boasted a number of father and son players, the most notable being Les Allen and his son Clive. An ever-present in the League and FA Cup in the 'double' winning season of 1960–61, Les Allen was a prolific goalscorer and hit five in an FA Cup game against Crewe. In 1986–87 Clive Allen scored 49 goals in all first-class matches to beat Jimmy Greaves's long-standing record.

FENWICK, TERRY. By the time Venables paid £550,000 in December 1987 to bring him to White Hart Lane, he had a total of 19 full England caps to his credit. A versatile player, he played at full-back, central defence, midfield and in the sweeper's role. Just when he seemed to have settled at right-back, he broke a leg in a Littlewoods Cup match at Old Trafford in March 1989. On recovery, he was loaned to Leicester City but was soon back at White Hart Lane and pushing for a first-team place. Within a month, he broke an ankle in the pre-match warm-up for an FA Cup match at Portsmouth. Leaving Spurs in August 1993 he is now manager of Portsmouth.

FEWEST DEFEATS. During Tottenham's Second Division championship winning season of 1919–20, the club went through the 42-match programme losing only four games. The first of these came in the 13th game of the season at Bury (1–2) after the club had won 11 and drawn one of the first 12 fixtures. The remaining three defeats were also away from home as Spurs went through their games at White Hart Lane undefeated.

FEYENOORD. Spurs have played the Dutch club on four occasions in the three European competitions. They first met in November 1961 in the first round of the European Cup. Spurs won in Holland 3–1 with Frank Saul scoring two of the goals and then were held 1–1 at home to win 4–2 on aggregate. The clubs' next meeting was in the UEFA final of 1974 when Feyenoord drew 2–2 at White Hart Lane before beating Spurs 2–0 on home soil to win the trophy 4–2 on aggregate. Ten years later the clubs met again in the same competition when Spurs gained revenge with a 6–2 aggregate victory in the second round of the competition. The last time they met was in the third round of the 1991–92 European Cup-winners' Cup, Spurs losing 1–0 on aggregate.

FIORUCCI CUP. On 27 April 1993, Spurs met Real Madrid and Internazionale for the Fiorucci Cup. Both games were played at White Hart Lane but were only of 45 minutes duration. Spurs went down 1–0 to Real Madrid and though they played out a goalless draw with Internazionale, they lost 6–5 on penalties.

FIRST DIVISION. Spurs have had five spells in the First Division. They lost their first-ever match in this division 3–1 at Sunderland on 1 September 1909 and continually battled against relegation until in 1914–15 they finished last and were relegated. Promoted in the next possible season of football, 1919–20, they played in the First Division for eight successive seasons in which they finished as runners-up in 1921–22. Following promotion in 1932–33, the club's third spell in the top flight was their shortest of just two seasons. Promoted again in 1949–50 the club embarked on their longest stay in Division One, playing 27 consecutive seasons and winning the League championship on two occasions and finishing runners-up three times. The club's last spell in the First Division was from 1978–79 to 1991–92 when the new FA Premier League took over.

FIRST LEAGUE MATCH. Spurs found themselves playing their first-ever Football League match on a Tuesday afternoon and that day was 1 September 1908. Their opponents were the FA Cup holders, Wolverhampton Wanderers, and a crowd of 20,000 turned out despite the torrential rain. Spurs recorded their first League victory 3–0, at the first attempt, Vivian Woodward scoring after just six minutes. The other goals were scored by Morris and again by Woodward.

FLOODLIGHTS. White Hart Lane switched on its floodlights for the first time on 29 September 1953 with a friendly against Racing Club de Paris. Spurs won 5–3 with Bennett (2), Duquemin, Burgess and Hutchinson scoring for the home side. The system was mounted on four corner poles (not pylons), each of them a few feet lower than the East Stand, with additional gantries on the two stand gables. It was because of these extra lamps that the ball and cockerel was moved to the East Stand gable, where it remains today, flanked by the lights. The first competitive match under floodlights was at The Dell on 1

October 1951 when Southampton Reserves played Spurs Reserves in a Football Combination match.

FOOTBALL COMBINATIONS. Spurs' first team took part in the first four seasons of the London Combination, from 1915–16 to 1918–19, the reserves taking over from 1919–20 when they became the first reserve club to win the Football Combination. The club's 1994–95 title win was their 19th – a record for the Football Combination.

FOOTBALL LEAGUE. Spurs joined the Second Division of the Football League in 1908 after 12 seasons in the First Division of the Southern League.

FOOTBALL LEAGUE CUP. For a time Spurs did not appear interested in the Football League Cup and even failed to participate during its early years. But once the final was booked for Wembley, their interest began to grow, although it took a few years before they finally lifted the trophy. The club's first match in the competition was on 14 September 1966 when they lost 1–0 against West Ham United at Upton Park. In a five-year spell from 1968–73, Spurs reached the semi-final on four occasions. In 1982 the trophy was renamed the Milk Cup and has subsequently been known as the Littlewoods Cup and the Rumbelows Cup. It is currently called the Coca-Cola Cup. Spurs have now won the trophy on two occasions, appearing in three finals.
Final Appearances:
1971 Aston Villa 0 Tottenham Hotspur 2 (*aet*) (Wembley)
1973 Norwich City 0 Tottenham Hotspur 1 (Wembley)
1982 Liverpool 3 Tottenham Hotspur 1 (*aet*) (Wembley)

FOOTBALLER OF THE YEAR. The Football Writers' Footballer of the Year award has been won by Tottenham players on a number of occasions. Past winners have been:
1958 Danny Blanchflower
1961 Danny Blanchflower
1973 Pat Jennings
1982 Steve Perryman
1987 Clive Allen
1992 Gary Lineker

1995 Jürgen Klinsmann
The Professional Football Association award for Player of the Year has gone to two Tottenham players:
1976 Pat Jennings
1987 Clive Allen

FOREMAN, GEORGE. An amateur with both Leyton and Walthamstow, Foreman played in the amateur international against Ireland before signing professional for West Ham United in 1939. Throughout the war years he was the Hammers' top scorer, but in 1944–45 he guested for Spurs and scored eight goals in five games. Signed in February 1946, he celebrated his transfer with both goals in a 2–0 win over Plymouth Argyle. Replaced by Charlie Rundle, he moved to inside-forward, but Len Duquemin then emerged and Foreman didn't make the first team again.

FORSTER, MATT. Signed from Northern Alliance club Newburn when only 19, he spent his first three seasons as reserve for the Cup final full-back Bob McDonald. Replacing him during the 1922–23 season, he appeared regularly in one of the full-back berths for the next six seasons. A solid and dependable full-back, he was never far away from international recognition and played for the Football League and for the Rest in an international trial. Unfortunately this may well have prevented him from earning the honours his consistent displays warranted.

FRANCIS, GERRY. Joining Queen's Park Rangers as a 13-year-old, he made his way up through the ranks, a member of one of the most successful youth sides ever at Loftus Road. He made his League debut coming on as a substitute in the 2–1 home defeat by Liverpool. Professional forms were signed in June 1969 and although 1969–70 saw Francis make only the occasional appearance it did see his first goal which came in the 3–1 win at Portsmouth in what was his full League debut. Despite the attractive football on offer at Loftus Road, promotion was not gained until 1972–73. The next three seasons were to prove to be amongst the most successful in the history of Queen's Park Rangers. In 1975–76 the *Match of the Day* cameras witnessed a goal from Francis in Rangers' 2–0 defeat of Liverpool that would eventually win the 'Goal of the Season' award. Having made his

England debut in October 1974, manager Don Revie handed the captaincy over to the QPR skipper with the statement that it was his for the next ten years. In the close season of 1979 he signed for his old friend Terry Venables at Crystal Palace for a fee of £465,000. When Venables returned to Loftus Road as manager the following season, he was closely followed by Francis at a knock-down price of £150,000. Twelve months later he joined Coventry City, assisting the 'Sky Blues' in their fight against relegation. He became player-manager of Exeter City when only 32 and experienced a nightmare start in management. The Devon side had one of their worst-ever seasons during his year in charge and finished bottom of the Third Division. Shortly afterwards he was sacked. He had a trial at Luton and then spent the 1984–85 season with Cardiff, Swansea and Portsmouth on a non-contract basis. He then joined Bristol Rovers and after two years he was offered the manager's chair. Hanging up his boots, he was rewarded by taking Rovers back to Division Two. He returned to Rangers in May 1991 but in November 1994 joined Spurs. In his first season he took the club to seventh in the Premier League and the semi-final of the FA Cup. In June 1995 he broke the club transfer record when he paid £4.5 million for Palace's Chris Armstrong.

G

GALVIN, TONY. After obtaining a Bachelor of Arts degree in Russian Studies at Hull University, he went on to Teacher Training College and played for Goole Town in the Northern Premier League. Signed in January 1978, his early progress was interrupted by a pelvic injury which sidelined him for almost a year and it wasn't until January 1981 that he sprang to prominence. Though still in pain, he scored in the FA Cup third round replay victory over Queen's Park Rangers and played an important role during the rest of that campaign that ended triumphantly at Wembley. He collected a second FA Cup winners' medal in 1982 and his star performances in the two legs of the 1984 UEFA Cup final confirmed him as a player for big occasions. Although he had been born in Huddersfield, Galvin qualified to play for the Republic of Ireland through his grandfather and he won his first cap against Holland in September 1982. He won 20 caps whilst with Spurs and a further nine when he moved to Sheffield Wednesday in 1987. He suffered more than his fair share of injuries at Hillsborough too, and two years later moved to Swindon Town where he was made assistant manager to Ossie Ardiles. He followed the little Argentinian to Newcastle United, but in February 1992 he was dismissed along with Ardiles in a boardroom reshuffle.

Paul Gascoigne

GASCOIGNE, PAUL. First associated with Newcastle United as a schoolboy he progressed through the ranks to make his League debut a month before turning professional. Quickly establishing himself as the most exciting talent of his generation, he was voted Young Player of the Year by the PFA in 1988. His sense of humour occasionally got him into trouble but in July 1988 Spurs manager Terry Venables signed Gazza for a British record fee of £2 million, knowing he could harness Gascoigne's talents without removing the impishness that delighted the British public. Within 11 days of his Spurs debut at Newcastle, where the Geordie fans pelted him with Mars Bars, he won his first full England cap, playing as substitute against Denmark. He was immediately hailed as the player around whom England should build its team for the 1990 World Cup. He was the undoubted star in England's march to the semi-finals. His televised tears when he realised a booking in the semi-final would rule him out of the final should England get there, endeared him to the nation, who in turn voted him BBC Television Sports Personality of the Year. He continued where he left off in 1990–91, steering Spurs almost single-handedly to the

FA Cup final. His day was ruined after only 15 minutes by a serious ligament injury, caused by a rash challenge on his part and he was carried off. The career-threatening damage to his cruciate ligament put his record £8.5 million move to Lazio in jeopardy. after taking a year to recover he eventually moved for £5.5 million to show the Italians what he could do. In the summer of 1995 he joined Scottish club Glasgow Rangers, helping them to a very successful season.

GAVIN, JOHNNY. By the time he joined Spurs in October 1954, Johnny Gavin had played over 200 League games for Norwich City and won four caps for the Republic of Ireland. He soon settled in at White Hart Lane and with his speed and strength, this diminutive winger became a great crowd favourite. After adding two more caps to his total in May 1955, he lost his place the following season to Sonny Walters and returned to Norwich as part of the deal that brought Maurice Norman to Spurs.

GIBBONS, JACK. One of the best amateur footballers of the 1940s, he made a goalscoring debut for Spurs at Sheffield Wednesday in September 1937. In 33 appearances that season, he scored 18 goals and collected the first of seven England amateur caps. He appeared regularly for Spurs during the war years and played for England against Wales in the wartime international in 1942. Spurs were hopeful he would stay at White Hart Lane after the war, but he moved up north to work and signed for Bradford Park Avenue. An amateur throughout his playing career, he made goalscoring seem simple, scoring 109 goals in all competitions from just 148 appearances.

GIBSON, TERRY. At his most effective in the penalty box, the 5ft 4in dasher showed all the qualities that once made him one of the hottest properties in local youth football. He made his League debut against Stoke City in December 1979 whilst still an apprentice. Signing professional forms the following month, he retained his place for two FA Cup ties with Manchester United before returning to the reserves. Despite one settled run of 19 games in early 1983, when he scored six goals, he was still unable to maintain a regular place at White Hart Lane and in August 1983 he moved to Coventry City. After 43 goals in 97 League games he

Alan Gilzean

was transferred to Manchester United but after a miserable 18 months in which he was never given the opportunity to prove himself, he returned to London with Wimbledon. He helped the Dons establish themselves in the top flight and played his part in their shock FA Cup victory over Liverpool in 1988.

GILZEAN, ALAN. He joined Tottenham in December 1964, a superb £72,500 signing from Dundee, with whom he had scored prolifically, helping them win the Scottish title and reach the European Cup semi-finals. He first played at White Hart Lane for a Scotland XI against Spurs in November 1964 when he scored twice in a memorial match for John White. At Dundee he had been an out-and-out centre-forward, but at Spurs he had to adapt his style to form deadly partnerships with Jimmy Greaves and later Martin Chivers. He won winners' medals in the 1967 FA Cup final, the 1971 and 1973 Football League Cup finals and the 1972 UEFA Cup final. His main strength was his amazing heading ability – not only powerful, but deft and delicate also. Whilst with Spurs he won 17 Scottish caps to add to the five he won with

Dundee, before he finished his career on the club's 1974 tour to Mauritius. He later played in South Africa and managed Southern League Stevenage Athletic before taking a job outside the game.

GLORY, GLORY, HALLELUJAH. The most individual and evocative of all English club tunes, it became established during Spurs' European Cup ties of the 1960s.

> Glory, Glory, Hallelujah
> Glory, Glory, Hallelujah
> Glory, Glory, Hallelujah
> And the Spurs go marching on.

(to the tune of *The Battle Hymn of the Republic*,1865)

GOALKEEPERS. Tottenham Hotspur FC has almost always been extremely well served by its goalkeepers and most of them have been highly popular with the supporters. Their first outstanding star was George Clawley. In the 1901 FA Cup final he was involved in a controversial incident when he dropped the ball and Sheffield United were awarded a goal – despite the evidence to suggest it had not crossed the line. John Eadon conceded an embarrassing seven goals on his debut as Spurs went down 7–5 at Middlesbrough on 13 February 1915. In recent years, Erik Thorstvedt also made an embarrassing debut in the 'live' televised clash with Nottingham Forest as he made a terrible gaffe in conceding the winning goal. Spurs have also had a number of goalscoring goalkeepers. In August 1967 Pat Jennings scored a goal with a long downfield kick in the 2–2 draw against Manchester United at Old Trafford in the Charity Shield, though John 'Tiny' Joyce remains the only goalkeeper to score for Spurs in a Football League game, netting against Bolton Wanderers on 10 April 1914. He also scored a penalty for Spurs in a tour match against Bayern Munich as did Ray Clemence against a Guernsey FA XI in April 1985. On 2 October 1965, Spurs provided both goalkeepers in the match between Northern Ireland and Scotland when Pat Jennings and Bill Brown faced each other. Tony Parks carved a permanent place for himself in Spurs' history with his second save in a shoot-out with Anderlecht in the 1984 UEFA Cup final, to win the trophy for Spurs. When Spurs were touring Canada in 1952, they were leading Saskatchewan 14–0 at half-time, so they lent Ted Ditchburn to the home team. He kept the score down. The result was 18–1. On 7 September 1985, Ray Clemence played his 1,000th senior game. It was a League match for Spurs against Newcastle United. The only other player at the time with as many appearances was his deputy Pat Jennings with 1,087 senior matches to his credit.

GOALS. The most goals Tottenham have ever scored in one game was their 13–2 victory against Crewe Alexandra in an FA Cup fourth round replay at White Hart Lane on 3 February 1960. Les Allen scored five, Bobby Smith four, Cliff Jones three and Tommy Harmer one. In the League, Spurs beat Everton 10–4 in 1958–59 and Bristol Rovers 9–0 in 1977–78.

GOALS – INDIVIDUAL. A number of players have scored five goals in a game for Spurs. The first was Kenny McKay, who netted five in Spurs' 6–2 win over the Royal Engineers in November 1898. Bill Joyce hit five in the final game of that season as Spurs beat Dartford 9–0 to finish third in the Thames and Medway League. Vivian Woodward scored five as West Ham United were beaten 10–0 in the semi-final of the Southern Charity Cup in 1905. On the opening day of the 1930–31 season, Ted Harper became the first Tottenham player to strike five in a Football League match as they beat Reading 7–1. It was another 27 years before the feat was ever repeated, the honour falling to Alfie Stokes who netted five as Spurs beat Birmingham City 7–1. The last person to score five goals was Les Allen in the 13–2 1960 FA Cup victory over Crewe Alexandra. There is an instance of a Tottenham player scoring seven goals, but it was during the war when Spurs played Luton Town, so does not officially count. The man who scored seven of Spurs' goals that day was Jack Rowley, then a Manchester United player guesting with the club. Also, during the club's 1952 tour of North America, Sid McClellan scored nine of Spurs' goals in the 18–1 win over the Saskatchewan FA XI.

GOALS – CAREER BEST. The highest goalscorer in the club's history is Jimmy Greaves who between season 1961–62 and the end of season 1969–70 had netted 266 goals for the club. These comprised of 220 in the League, 32 in the FA Cup, five in the

Football League Cup and nine in Europe. On top of this, Greaves scored 40 goals in other games to bring his grand total to 306 in just 420 appearances.

GOALS – SEASON. The club's highest League goalscorer in any one season remains Jimmy Greaves who scored 37 League goals as Spurs finished second in the First Division in 1962–63. The season's highest tally for all matches is the 49 goals achieved by Clive Allen in 1986–87. Thirty-three were scored in the League, 12 in the Football League Cup and four in the FA Cup.

GOALSCORING RECORDS. In 1900–01, Spurs' Alexander 'Sandy' Brown became the first man to score in every round of the FA Cup in one season and in scoring 15 goals he established a record for the most goals in one competition – a record that still stands. Clive Allen is the record holder for the most goals in the Football League Cup in a season. He scored 12 times during the 1986–87 campaign.

GOUGH, RICHARD. By the time of his £700,000 transfer from Dundee United in August 1986, he was a Scottish international with 26 caps to his credit, the star of Scotland's disappointing World Cup campaign and Scottish PFA Player of the Year for 1986. Appointed captain at Charlton on New Year's Day 1987, he missed only two games that season and led the club to the FA Cup final. A tall, commanding player, he had the skill to retain possession of the ball and distribute it accurately, a player who always seemed to have time to play his way out of trouble. Having added eight more caps to his total and played for the Football League against the Rest of the World in the League's centenary match at Wembley he looked to have a long and illustrious career ahead of him at Spurs. However, his family were unable to settle in London and in October 1987 Spurs reluctantly allowed him to move to Glasgow Rangers for £1.5 million. Alongside his former Spurs team-mate Graham Roberts, he helped Rangers win the Skol Cup in his first season at Ibrox and has gone on to win numerous honours with the Scottish club. One of the most accomplished defenders in the game, he now has 61 Scottish caps to his name.

GREAVES, JIMMY. The greatest goalscorer in Spurs' history and arguably the history of British football, he made his Football League debut against Spurs with Chelsea on the opening day of the 1957–58 season. He scored then in a 1–1 draw, as he did on all of his debut days. It was the first of 357 goals in the Football League, all of them in the First Division. After only six League games for Chelsea, he made his debut for the England Under-23s and scored twice against Bulgaria at Stamford Bridge. He stayed with Chelsea until June 1961 when he left to join AC Milan. He had actually signed a contract nine months earlier, but it was subject to the Italians lifting an embargo on foreign players. His full England debut and first goal had come in a 4–1 defeat in Peru in May 1959. His goalscoring debut for Milan came in a friendly against Botafoga. Despite the tough, defensive tactics of the Italian League, he scored nine goals in 14 matches, but not able to stomach the petty disciplines the Italians imposed on their players he made clear his desire to return to English football. In December 1961 he joined Spurs for £99,999 – Bill Nicholson refusing to pay a six-figure fee! He responded on his debut with a hat-trick at home to Blackpool, starting with a superb scissors-kick. He won an FA Cup winners' medal in his first season, scoring the opening goal at Wembley. He scored twice in the European Cup-winners' Cup final the following year and ended that 1962–63 season with Spurs' highest-scorer-in-a-season record with 37 League goals. When he topped the First Division scoring chart in 1964–65 he became the first player to do so for three consecutive seasons. A serious illness in 1965–66 meant that he was unable to reach full fitness for the World Cup finals that summer. In his time with Spurs he won 42 caps and scored 28 goals – his overall record being 44 goals in 57 appearances. In March 1970, he left Spurs to join West Ham United as part of the deal that took Martin Peters to White Hart Lane. He scored twice on his debut for the Hammers, but retired at the end of the 1970–71 season, when still only 31 years old. In October 1972 a crowd of 45,799 turned out to pay tribute in his testimonial match against Feyenoord. He responded in the only way he knew, scoring after only three minutes! He later played non-League football, but fell victim to alcoholism, a problem that threatened his very existence. Rehabilitation was followed by new stardom as a TV pundit, a role in which he revels.

Jimmy Greaves

GREENFIELD, GEORGE. One of the finest inside-forwards to play for Spurs since the First World War, he made only 12 appearances in his first season with the club. He appeared in the first three matches of the 1932–33 campaign, but missed the next five before being recalled to the side. Spurs then won nine and drew two of their next 11 matches with Greenfield being hailed as the best schemer in the country. Unfortunately he broke his leg in the penultimate game of that sequence, a 2–2 draw at Fulham. Though he managed to return for six games in 1934–35, he was never able to overcome the injury and joined the ground staff.

75

GRENADIER GUARDS. To celebrate promotion in 1932–33 Spurs engaged the band of the Grenadier Guards to play at their first hoe match of the new season against Wolverhampton Wanderers on Monday, 28 August. Kick-off was scheduled for 7.30 p.m. but unfortunately the servicemen were unavailable for an evening performance, so Spurs changed the kick-off time to the afternoon. Both the band and team played well, Spurs winning 4–0 with two goals apiece from O'Callaghan and Hunt, but many fans were unable to attend – 20,953 compared to the season's average of 34,579.

GRIMSDELL, ARTHUR. An England schoolboy international centre-forward before signing for his home-town club Watford, he was converted to a centre-half. Joining Spurs in March 1912, he played his first few games at centre-half but when Peter McWilliam was appointed manager some nine months later, he was immediately installed at left-half. Strong in defence and attack, Arthur Grimsdell was one of the best-ever all-round wing-halves. By the age of 19 he was already close to England honours, playing in the international trial match of November 1913. One of the first Spurs players to enlist, Grimsdell was lost to Spurs for most of the hostilities, but when he returned to White Hart Lane in 1919 he had developed from a slightly built youth into a powerfully built man determined to succeed. He played in the international trial of April 1919 and for England in the Victory international against Scotland where he demonstrated his powerful long-range shooting with two goals. In Spurs' first League season after the war, he captained the club to the Second Division title, scoring 14 goals with his long-range efforts. His most obvious attributes were his never-say-die attitude and his non-stop running. He was captain of the team when Spurs won the FA Cup in 1921. Grimsdell was immovable from the team except when injured and in October 1925 with Spurs on top of the First Division he broke his leg at Leicester City. He did not return until April 1927 but was not the force he had been

OGDEN'S CIGARETTES.

A. GRIMSDELL,
TOTTENHAM HOTSPUR.

before injury and, two years later, Spurs released one of the greatest players ever to have served the club.

GROUNDSMEN. When Spurs won the FA Cup in 1921, their groundsman was John Over and it was he who carried the Cup round the ground the following week. Four decades earlier he had laid out the pitch for the first England v Australia Test match at Kennington Oval and joined Spurs from Edmonton Cricket Club. While he remained in charge of the White Hart Lane pitch, no one was allowed to set foot on it. Even the stars like Jimmy Seed and Arthur Grimsdell would be disciplined if they chose to ignore the rule – it was even rumoured that Over had doubts about them trespassing on his pitch on a Saturday afternoon. When he died, his son Will took over as head groundsman.

GUEST PLAYERS. The 'guest' system was used by all clubs during the two wars. Although at times it was abused almost beyond belief (in that some sides that opposed Spurs had ten or 11 'guests'!) it normally worked sensibly and effectively to the benefit of players, clubs and supporters alike. The most distinguished players to 'guest' for Tottenham Hotspur were four England internationals: Vic Woodley, the Chelsea goalkeeper; Jack Rowley, the Manchester United centre-forward; and two of England's greatest post-war inside-forwards, Middles-brough's Wilf Mannion and Ivor Broadis, who enjoyed his best days with Manchester City and Newcastle United.

H

HALL, WILLIE. Signed from Notts County to replace George Greenfield, who had broken a leg, Willie Hall was a clever ball-playing inside-forward who worked well with his winger. He made his Spurs debut against his old club in December 1932 and at the end of the season they were promoted to the First Division. Notts County had very sensibly inserted a clause whereby they received £500 if Hall was capped for England. Within a year Hall had made his England debut playing against France and went on to win ten caps. He also scored nine goals at international level, a remarkable record for someone not known as a goalscorer. Five of these came against Northern Ireland at Old Trafford in November 1938 and included possibly the fastest ever international hat-trick. In addition to his caps, he played three times for the Football League. Sadly a serious leg disease forced him to retire and subsequently the lower parts of both legs were amputated.

WILLS'S CIGARETTES

G. W. HALL (TOTTENHAM HOTSPUR)

HANDLEY, CHARLIE. A hard-working forward, Charlie 'Tich' Handley learned his football whilst serving in the Army during the First World War. Never able to settle in one position during his career at Spurs, he had to compete with the likes of Dimmock, Elkes, Osborne and Seed. Nevertheless, he turned in many useful performances for Spurs and scored hat-tricks in the club's FA Cup run of 1922–23 when Worksop were beaten 9–0 and Manchester United 4–0. Released in April 1929 he spent a season with Swansea Town before he eventually went to Switzerland to help his former Spurs colleague, Bert Smith, as coach at Berne.

HARMER, TOMMY. Affectionately nicknamed 'The Charmer' he was one of the most entertaining players to wear a Spurs shirt. Slight of build, various schemes were tried in his early days to encourage him to gain weight, yet on the pitch he was a heavyweight unrivalled for sheer wizardry on the ball. However, his individualistic skills did not suit the 'push and run' style that brought the club success in the early '50s. There is no doubt that it held him back and although he won an England 'B' cap against Holland in March 1952, it was only after Eddie Baily's departure in January 1956 that he was able to gain a regular first-team place. He flourished in a creative midfield partnership with Danny Blanchflower which helped Spurs finish as first Division runners-up in 1956–57, during which he scored 17 League goals. Held in high affection at White Hart Lane, legend has it that he made nine goals and scored one in Spurs' 10–4 annihilation of Everton in October 1958. Sadly, though, he did not fit in with Bill Nicholson's plans for the 1960–61 season and with the first team doing so well, he was transferred to Watford in October 1960. Two years later he moved to Chelsea and scored the goal that won Tommy Docherty's young side promotion to the top flight in 1962–63.

HARPER, TED. A prolific goalscorer throughout his career, Ted Harper played with Whitstable and Sheppey before joining Blackburn Rovers where 43 goals in a season won him an England cap against Scotland in April 1926. He moved to Sheffield Wednesday and it was from the Owls that Spurs signed him. Ted Harper scored 83 goals in only 78 senior matches for Tottenham. His record could have been even better, but because of his reputation, he often received some rough handling from opponents and therefore missed matches through injury. In 1930–31 he scored 36 goals in only 30 League appearances to set a new Spurs record. If he hadn't been injured at Swansea and had to miss six of the last eight matches, he would undoubtedly have scored more and, more importantly, Spurs would probably have gained promotion instead of finishing third behind Everton and West Bromwich Albion. When Harper was injured, he was replaced by George Hunt and because he did so well, Harper was unable to recover his place. Allowed to move to Preston North End, he showed he was still as sharp as ever by scoring 43 goals in 1932–33. This meant that he had the enviable record of having scored most goals in a season for three different clubs.

HARTLEY, JAMES. He arrived at Spurs in the summer of 1897 after gaining experience with Dumbarton, Sunderland, Burnley and Lincoln City. He scored both Spurs' goals on his debut in a 2–0 win over Gravesend United. Losing his place to Bob Tannahill the following season, he returned to Lincoln.

HAT-TRICK HEROES. Spurs' hat-trick hero has to be Frank Osborne who, during the 1925–26 season, hit three consecutive hat-tricks to become the first player ever to achieve the feat. His first hat-trick came in the 3–1 win at White Hart Lane over Liverpool in October 1925. The following week he hit all three Spurs goals in the 5–3 defeat at Leicester City and seven days later at White Hart Lane, West Ham United were beaten 4–2 with Osborne scoring three more goals. Another hat-trick hero was Jimmy Greaves, who hit three goals on his debut against Blackpool in December 1961 as Spurs won 5–2. Colin Lee also hit a hat-trick on his debut – in fact, he scored four goals as Spurs beat Bristol Rovers 9–0 in October 1977. Alfie Conn's one League appearance as a substitute was followed by his full debut at Newcastle United on 11 January 1975. He celebrated in style with a hat-trick in Spurs' best victory of the season. Five other players have scored hat-tricks on their debut for the club, though not in the Football League. They are: Harry Rainbird v West Norwood, 1902; Jimmy Reid v London Caledonians, 1906; Max Seeburg v Ostend, 1907; Almer Hall v Corinthians, 1934; and Les Bennett v Watford, 1939. Spurs' Willie Hall scored five goals for England against Ireland on 16 November 1938 including the fastest international hat-trick achieved in just three and a half minutes!

HAZARD, MICKEY. Sunderland-born, this highly talented mid-field player spent most of his time at White Hart Lane in the shadow of Glenn Hoddle. When Hoddle was absent he would come into his own but when they played together Hazard was much less effective. However, he was a key member of the squad and won his first major honour, an FA Cup winners' medal, when he played in both games of the replayed 1982 Cup final. Two years later he played a major role in the club's UEFA Cup success, appearing in the final after his brilliant goal had helped Spurs defeat Hajduk Split in the semi-final. He moved to Chelsea for £310,000 in September 1985 in an attempt to play regular first-team football. Never really able to command a regular first-team place at Stamford Bridge he moved to Portsmouth in January 1990 for £100,000. He lost his place at Fratton Park after only two months and had his career rescued by Ossie Ardiles at Swindon Town. Under both Ardiles and his successor Glenn Hoddle, Hazard finally found the consistency which had previously eluded him. In November 1993 he returned to White Hart Lane for a second spell for the cut-price fee of £50,000.

HENRY, RON. Spotted as a teenage outside-left when stationed at Woolwich during his National Service, he was converted into a left-half and made his senior debut at centre-half against Huddersfield Town in 1955, before becoming a left-back. It was an injury to Mel Hopkins, who broke his nose in an international for Wales against Scotland, that brought him into the Spurs team to stay. He missed only one of the next 188 games during which he formed an excellent full-back partnership with Peter Baker. He won a League championship medal in 1961, FA Cup winners' medals in 1961 and 1962, and a European Cup-winners' Cup medal in 1963. His consistency for Spurs was rewarded with an England cap against France in February 1963, but in what was manager Alf Ramsey's first match, England were hammered 5–1 and Henry never got another chance at the top level. The only goal of his 14-year White Hart Lane career was a speculative 35-yarder against eventual champions Manchester United and amazing and delighting the Spurs crowd. Troubled by a cartilage injury in the later stages, Ron Henry moved into coaching the Spurs juniors following his retirement from playing.

HINTON, BILL. Signed from Bolton Wanderers, where he played in only 36 first-team games in four years, he made his Spurs debut in a 3–0 win over his old club at the start of the 1924–25 season. An ever-present during that campaign, he conceded just 43 goals and kept 13 clean sheets. Unfortunately, illness struck early the following season and, after struggling through 18 games, he did not play another game at senior level.

HITCHINS, ARTHUR. When he signed professional forms in January 1935, Arthur Hitchins was a full-back. Following 12 months in the reserves, he was sent to the Northfleet nursery, returning to White Hart Lane as a half-back. Yet when he made his first-team debut against Plymouth Argyle in October 1937, it was at centre-half. By the end of the following season he was being tipped as a future England international, but his career was destroyed by the war.

HODDLE, GLENN. One of the most gifted footballers ever to have played for the club, he signed professional forms in April 1975 after overcoming a bad knee injury in his teens. He won England Youth caps before making his League debut as a substitute against Norwich City in August 1975. His first full season in the Spurs team was marred by relegation, but he soon helped them back into the top flight. Having won his first England Under-21 cap against Wales in December 1976, he won seven more and played twice for the England 'B' team before making his full international debut against Bulgaria in 1979 with a goal. In 1979–80 he scored 22 times for Tottenham and at the end of the season was the winner of the PFA Young Player of the Year award. He won FA Cup winners' medals in 1981 (when his free-kick resulted in an equaliser) and 1982 (when he scored in both games) and played in the losing team of 1987. He won a total of 12 Under-21 caps, two for England 'B' and 44 full caps with Spurs. In the 1987 close season he signed for the French League club AS Monaco. Winning nine more caps, he helped Monaco to the French title in 1987–88 and was voted best foreign player in the League. Unfortunately, he was then troubled by persistent knee injuries which all but ended his career. In December 1990 he

Glenn Hoddle

bought up his contract and returned to England to sign for Chelsea on a non-contract basis. Without ever playing a game he left in March 1991 to embark on a career in management. Succeeding Ossie Ardiles at Swindon Town he took them to promotion in 1993 via the play-offs. In June 1993 he took over the reins at Chelsea. An emphatic 4–0 win over Tottenham Hotspur saw them clinch the prestigious pre-season Makita Tournament. Not only the first victory for an English club for four years, but also Chelsea's first trophy for 22 years! The following season he took them to the FA Cup final, where they lost 4–0 to 'double' winners Manchester United. Though they were distinct underdogs, they were the only side to have beaten United twice in the League. In 1994–95 they progressed to the semi-finals of the European Cup-winners' Cup before going out 4–3 to the eventual winners, Real Zaragoza. Signing Ruud Guillit from Sampdoria and Mark Hughes from Manchester United, Glenn Hoddle is one of the country's most enlightened managers.

HODGE, STEVE. A busy left-sided midfield player, he made his League debut for Nottingham Forest in the final game of the 1981–82 season. In March 1983 he made an England Under-21 debut against Greece and had won five caps at that level before joining Aston Villa for £450,000 in August 1985. At Villa Park he won 11 full England caps and was a regular member of England's 1986 World Cup team. With Villa struggling at the wrong end of the table, he took the chance of a £650,000 move to Tottenham, where he marked his Boxing Day debut with a goal against West Ham United in a 4–0 win. Despite helping Spurs to that season's FA Cup final, he never really settled in London and in August 1988 he returned to Nottingham Forest for a fee of £575,000. Back at the City Ground he won League Cup winners' medals in 1989 and 1990 and came on as a substitute during the 1991 FA Cup final against Spurs. Brian Clough sold him to Leeds United in the summer of 1991 for £900,000. Despite being hampered by injury problems, he scored some vital goals and made enough appearances to earn a League championship medal as Leeds lifted the title in 1992. Following a short loan spell with Derby County, he joined Queen's Park Rangers for £300,000 in October 1994.

HOLMES, JIMMY. When he made his League debut for Coventry City in January 1972, Jimmy Holmes had already won his first full cap for Eire! He was called on as a substitute against Austria in May 1971, becoming the youngest ever international for the Republic. He joined Spurs for £120,000 on transfer deadline day in March 1977, following a serious injury to John Gorman. Unable to prevent Spurs being relegated, he proved over the next two seasons to be an elegant defender of outstanding ability. Collecting his twelfth cap as a Spurs player against Bulgaria in Sofia in May 1979, Holmes broke his leg and never played for Spurs again. He was allowed to move to Vancouver Whitecaps of the North American Soccer League. After almost two years there, he returned to England and played on a non-contract basis for Leicester City, Brentford and Torquay United. He later made a new career for himself as a member of the West Midlands police force.

HOLLOWBREAD, JOHN. Signed from non-League Enfield in 1952, he demonstrated his patience by waiting six years before making his League debut. It was not a happy start for him as Spurs lost 5–0 at Blackburn. However, he kept his place for the rest of the 1958–59 season and turned in some brave performances as Spurs fought to avoid relegation. But in the summer of 1959, Spurs bought Bill Brown from Dundee and Hollowbread returned to the reserves. Though several clubs were keen to sign him, Bill Nicholson refused to let him leave. He had another long run in the first team in 1963–64 and this heightened his appetite for senior action. With the signing of Pat Jennings on the horizon, he left to join Southampton, but after only 36 games for the Saints he suffered a serious knee injury that forced his retirement.

HOME MATCHES. Spurs' best home wins are the 13–2 rout of Crewe Alexandra in a fourth round FA Cup replay on 3 February 1960 and the 10–4 win against Everton in the First Division match played on 11 October 1958. Spurs' worst home defeat is 6–0, a scoreline inflicted upon them by Sunderland in 1914–15 and Arsenal in 1934–35. Spurs have scored nine goals in a home match on five occasions: Worksop Town 9–0 (FA Cup 1922–23), Port Vale 9–3 (Division Two 1931–32), Tranmere Rovers 9–1 (FA Cup 1952–53), Nottingham Forest 9–2 (Division One 1962–63) and Bristol Rovers 9–0 (Division Two 1977–78).

HOME SEASONS. Tottenham Hotspur have gone through a complete League season with an undefeated home record on three occasions – 1919–20, 1932–33, and 1964–65. The club's highest number of home wins in a League season is 19. This was achieved in 1919–20 from 21 matches as they won the Second Division championship.

HOOPER, PERCY. Percy Hooper was reserve goalkeeper with Islington Corinthians when Spurs' regular reserve 'keeper Alan

Taylor was injured. Asked to stand in, he impressed and was sent along to the Northfleet nursery, later signing professional forms. He made his debut at the end of the 1934–35 season but his real chance came the following term and by the outbreak of the Second World War he was Spurs' first-choice 'keeper. His appearances for Spurs diminished as the hostilities went on and his absence allowed the great Ted Ditchburn to step in as the club's future number one. Early in 1947 he moved to Swansea Town.

HOPKINS, MEL. Growing up in a Rhondda rugby stronghold, Mel Hopkins had to form his own team to get a game of soccer. Later playing for the Ystrad Boys' Club in Glamorgan he was given the chance to join the ground staff of both Manchester United and Spurs – he chose Spurs. Highly rated by Spurs boss Arthur Rowe, he was given his League debut as a 17-year-old at Derby in October 1952. By the mid-'50s he was recognised as one of the best full-backs in the country. He made his international debut for Wales in April 1956 and immediately became an automatic choice. The highlight of his international career was the 1958 World Cup finals when Wales reached the quarter-finals. In November 1959, the Welshman's nose was smashed horrifically in a collision with Ian St John at Hampden Park, leaving Ron Henry to take his place at left-back. Though he remained at White Hart Lane for a further five years, he was never able to get back into the team on a regular basis. He later moved to Brighton and played a sterling role in that season's Fourth Division championship triumph.

HOTSPUR FC. The club's name of Hotspur was inspired by the historical Harry Hotspur familiar from the plays of William Shakespeare (the Hotspur family being the Percys, Dukes of Northumberland who owned land around Tottenham in the 1880s). Harry Hotspur himself acquired his name from his frequent use of spurs when riding and it is thought that the team's ball and cockerel emblem is probably also related to this idea, as fighting cocks were once fitted out with miniature Spurs. It is widely recorded that the early Hotspur team had no headquarters of their own until 1886 and so the committee had to meet under a gaslight lamp-post on Tottenham High Road, very close to the present ground. During the week the blue and white striped Hotspur goalposts were stored at Northumberland Park railway station and the players had to cross the Great Eastern railway to reach the Marshes. In 1885 Tottenham was added to their title and a year later they set up headquarters at the Red House, 748 High Road, in the building later to become the offices of White Hart Lane.

HOWE, LES. A fine all-round footballer, Les Howe was an extremely versatile player. Probably best remembered as a right-half, he actually played in every position in his 16 years of service with Spurs. After making his League debut on Boxing Day 1930 he did not get an extended run in the side until October 1932 when he played most of his matches at outside-right. A regular in the Spurs side in the early war years, an injury in September 1945 led to serious complications and he decided to retire from the first-class game.

HOWELLS, DAVID. He joined Tottenham Hotspur in July 1984 on a YTS scheme and signed professional forms just six months later. Having waited over a year for his Football League debut, he scored the winning goal in a 2–1 victory at Sheffield Wednesday in February 1986. He started his career as a forward, but settled into the Spurs side in a defensive midfield role, winning selection for the Football League against the Irish League in November 1990. Promoted to the England 'B' squad in January 1991, he was unfortunately forced to withdraw because of injury. That injury problem threatened to keep him out of Spurs 1991 FA Cup run but he recovered just in time to play in the semi-final defeat of Arsenal and then the final itself against Nottingham Forest. Now having played over 200 first-team games, Howells is an essential member of the Spurs side.

HUGHES, TED. When he was signed from Everton in July 1899, Ted Hughes was already a Welsh international although he had only made eight appearances for the Merseysiders. He added a further 12 caps to his international haul, making 14 in total and became one of the most important and influential figures in Spurs' rise to League status. He slowly began to establish himself in the team, but his real breakthrough came when he replaced

Spurs captain James McNaught early in the 1901 FA Cup run. He played so well that McNaught was never able to regain his place and it was Hughes who collected a winners' medal. A tireless worker with a great shot, he remained with Spurs until early in the 1907–08 season when he joined Clyde.

HUGHTON, CHRIS. He signed for Spurs in June 1979, after completing his training as a lift engineer. In his younger days he was a winger but was successfully converted to a full-back, capable of playing on either flank, although naturally right-footed. He made his first-team debut in the 2–1 Football League Cup defeat of Manchester United in August 1979 and won his first international cap shortly after. Qualifying to play for the Republic of Ireland through his mother, he went on to make 51 appearances in his career at White Hart Lane. He was a member of the 1981 and 1982 FA Cup winning teams and scored a couple of goals as Spurs made their way into the 1984 UEFA Cup final. His great service to the club was recognised with a free transfer in June 1990 and although he was in demand with several clubs, it was not until December that he decided to join West Ham United on a permanent basis following a loan spell. After helping the Hammers with promotion from the Second Division in 1990–91 he later joined Brentford in the new First Division but a knee injury forced him to retire in April 1993.

HULME, JOE. A goalscoring winger, Joe Hulme won three League championship medals and FA Cup winners' medals with Arsenal before moving to Huddersfield Town. His last game for the Yorkshire side was in the 1938 FA Cup final against Preston North End. Appointed Spurs manager in 1946, he had limited success at White Hart Lane. The club lost an FA Cup semi-final in 1948 against Blackpool, but he assembled most of the side which won the League championship after he left.

HUMPHREYS, PERCY. A regular goalscorer, Percy Humphreys started his career with Queen's Park Rangers in the Southern League before moving to Notts County. Here he played for the Football League against the Scottish League and for England against Scotland. After six seasons he moved to Leicester Fosse, but after just 26 games in which he scored 19 goals he was transferred to Chelsea. Within months he had lost his first-team place and joined Spurs who were struggling in their first season in Division One. His goalscoring talents were crucial, not just for Spurs, but for Chelsea also. In the final match of the season, Spurs played Chelsea; if Bristol City won their last game (which they did) the losers would be relegated. Spurs won 2–1 and it was Humphreys' goal that sent his former team-mates down to the Second Division.

HUNDRED GOALS. Spurs have scored more than 100 League goals in a season on four occasions. The highest total is 115 goals, scored in 1960–61 when they won the First Division championship. In 1962–63 they scored 111 goals and 104 in 1956–57, finishing runners-up in the First Division on both occasions. In 1919–20, Spurs scored 102 goals when winning the Second Division title.

HUNT, GEORGE. Known as the 'Chesterfield Tough', George Hunt was signed by manager Percy Smith in June 1930. A ball-playing centre-forward, he held the club's aggregate goalscoring record until the advent of Bobby Smith. He made his League debut against Stoke City in September 1930 but had to wait until the following March before he made the team again. Deputising for Ted Harper, Hunt netted five goals in eight games but Spurs lost six of these games and just missed out on promotion. However, Smith persevered with Hunt and in 1932–33 his 33 goals helped

CARRERAS CIGARETTES

G. HUNT

Spurs back into Division One. Around this time he won three England caps, the first against Italy in March 1933. Hunt's solo dashes through the heart of the opposing defences thrilled the White Hart Lane crowds, but after Jack Tresadern was appointed Spurs manager he was less a part of the Tottenham team. He was transferred to Arsenal in October 1937 but after only six months he moved to Bolton Wanderers. A regular for the Trotters during the war he helped them win the League Cup North in 1945.

Finishing his playing career with Sheffield Wednesday, he than returned to Burnden Park where he spent 20 years on the coaching staff.

HUNTER, ALEX. Having made his name with Scottish amateur club Queen's Park, he signed for Spurs as reserve to the regular choice goalkeeper Bill Jacques. It was following an injury to Jacques in February 1921 that Hunter was pitched into the Spurs first team. He performed so impressively that even when Jacques was fit. Hunter retained his place and won an FA Cup winners' medal two months later. It was a swift rise to fame but, unfortunately for Hunter, it was followed by an equally dramatic fall. After only 11 games of the 1921–22 season, Jacques won his place back and Hunter was allowed to move to Wigan Borough.

HUNTER, PETER. First playing for Spurs in 1894, Peter Hunter was a prolific goalscorer. Almost ever-present throughout the two most important seasons in the club's short history, he had the honour of scoring Spurs' opening FA Cup goal. Unfortunately his commitment to Spurs' plunge into professionalism probably helped end his career with the club, for there was no place for him when Willie Newbigging was signed from Lanark County in 1896.

I

ILEY, JIM. Signed from Sheffield United for £16,000 in August 1957 to replace Tony Marchi, he found it difficult to settle with Spurs and after only 12 appearances he found himself in the reserves. Toward the end of his first season he recovered his form, got back in the first team and collected an England Under-23 cap against Wales in April 1958. A creative wing-half, he might have had a long career at White Hart Lane if he had not been paired with Danny Blanchflower. Though there were a few occasions when the Yorkshire-born Iley was preferred to Danny, it came as no surprise in August 1959 when Bill Nicholson allowed him to join Nottingham Forest. He spent just over three years at the City Ground before joining Newcastle United where he enjoyed the best period of his career. In January 1969 he became player-manager of Peterborough United and went on to manage Barnsley, Blackburn Rovers, Bury and Exeter City before joining the coaching staff at Charlton Athletic.

INJURIES. The risk of serious injury is an ever-present threat in the game of football and all professional players expect to miss games through injury at some point in their careers. Notable Spurs casualties in recent years have ranged from Dave Mackay, who broke his left leg twice in 1964, but continued to play for another eight years (sometimes in great pain), to Paul Gascoigne, whose knee injury became a headline story when it threatened his transfer to Lazio in 1992. However, not every injury is sustained on the pitch of course: in 1964 Spurs' Alan Mullery missed England's tour of Brazil after he ricked his back cleaning his teeth!

INTERNATIONAL CAPS. The first Tottenham player ever to be capped was inside-forward John L. Jones, who played for Wales against Ireland on 19 February 1898.

INTERNATIONAL CAPS – MOST. Tottenham's most capped player is Pat Jennings, who represented Northern Ireland 75 times while he was at White Hart Lane.

J

JACQUES, BILL. He first found fame in a Gravesend team that included future England international Charlie Buchan before joining Coventry City in 1911. A brave, consistent goalkeeper, he joined Spurs in 1914 and made his debut against Everton in the first match of the last pre-war season. He played through the war years and when normal football resumed in 1919–20 he was an ever-present as the club won the Second Division title, keeping 18 clean sheets. An injury against West Bromwich in February 1921 caused him to miss out on an FA Cup medal that year as his place was taken by Alex Hunter. By October he had recovered his first-team place but in late 1922 he became ill, the symptoms forcing his retirement in early 1923. Two years later Bill died, aged only 36.

JENNINGS, PAT. At his peak, Pat Jennings was the best 'keeper in the world and a candidate among the best of all time. Having played Gaelic football for North Down Schools, he turned to football with Newry Town's junior club, Newry United. After a season with the juniors and six months with Newry Town he signed for Watford for £6,000 in May 1963. Thirteen months later he was on his way to White Hart Lane as Spurs boss Bill Nicholson paid Watford £27,000. In a 13-year spell at Tottenham, Jennings won an FA Cup winners' medal against Chelsea in 1967,

Pat Jennings

two League Cup winners' medals against Aston Villa and Norwich City in 1971 and 1973 respectively, a UEFA Cup winners' medal won by beating Wolves in 1972 as well as being named PFA Player of the Year in 1976. He went on to set a record number of appearances for Spurs, a figure bettered only by Steve Perryman. He was awarded the MBE for his services to the game in the 1976 Queen's Birthday Honours list. His achievements were also honoured by Spurs with a testimonial against Arsenal in November 1976. He also managed a goal for Spurs – a long downfield punt – in the 2–2 draw against Manchester United at Old Trafford in the 1967 FA Charity Shield game. Rarely injured, he did succumb to a serious ankle injury in 1976–77 and during his enforced absence Spurs were relegated! Even worse, manager Burkinshaw allowed Jennings to join rivals Arsenal, managed by his former Spurs boss and international colleague, Terry Neill. By the time of his transfer he had represented Northern Ireland 66 times as a Spurs player. He spent eight seasons at Highbury, making over 300 senior appearances, winning another FA Cup winners' medal in 1979, runners-up medals in 1978 and 1980, a European Cup-winners' Cup medal, also in 1980, as well as appearing in another 44 internationals. In May 1985 he was granted a second testimonial, this time against Spurs. He was on the verge of retiring but returned to White Hart Lane as goal-keeping cover for Ray Clemence, but also to keep fit for Northern Ireland, being needed for the 1986 World Cup finals. He won a further nine caps in his second spell at Spurs, giving him a world record total of 119. The conclusion of the World Cup saw Jennings officially retire, though later that year he did captain the Rest of the World XI against the Americas in a FIFA/UNICEF charity match.

JONES, CHRIS. Born in Jersey, the popular Channel Islander made his debut at the start of the 1974–75 season in place of Martin Chivers, but after the club had suffered three successive defeats, he was consigned to the reserves. He returned towards the end of the season to play alongside Chivers as Spurs battled to avoid relegation. Good in the air, he would find his way to the flanks, from which he would send in viciously dipping shots and crosses. He was also something of an unlucky player, his shots seeming to rebound from the woodwork with regularity. Though he was in contention for a first-team spot for five years he never stretched his end-of-season goal tally into double figures and when Archibald and Crooks arrived in the summer of 1980, the competition proved too much for him. He was transferred to Manchester City for £110,000 but after only three League games returned to London with Crystal Palace. He later played for Charlton, Orient and St Albans before returning home to Jersey to manage the St Peters club.

JONES, CLIFF. He was born into a football family: his father Ivor had been an inter-war international, his brother Bryn played for Swansea, Newport and Bournemouth, and his uncle Bryn had been transferred from Wolves to Arsenal for a British record fee just before the Second World War. He first came to prominence when Swansea defeated Manchester to win the Schools Shield. Having signed for Swansea Town in 1952, he was already a Welsh international when Spurs paid £35,000 for his signature in February 1958 – a record fee for a winger. Not long after arriving at White Hart Lane, he fractured a leg in a pre-season training collision with Peter Baker, but survived this setback and on his return to action in December 1958, he began to give value for money. At his peak, he was unquestionably world-class and became one of the most popular figures in Tottenham's history, thrilling the supporters with his courage, pace and goalscoring feats. A key member of the famous team that won the 'double' in 1960–61, the FA Cup in 1961–62 and the European Cup-winners' Cup in 1962–63, he picked up another winners' medal in the 1967 FA Cup final, as the first non-playing substitute. Throughout his career at White Hart Lane, he continued to represent Wales and added another 41 caps to the 16 he had won with Swansea. In October 1968 his great service to Spurs was recognised with a £5,000 cut-price transfer to Fulham, where he won his final two caps.

JONES, ERNIE. Ernie 'Alphabet' Jones turned professional with Bolton Wanderers, although he failed to make their League side. Returning to his home-town club of Swansea during the Second World War, he quickly built a reputation as a fast, direct, attacking winger. Moving to Spurs in June 1947, he only spent two full seasons at White Hart Lane before losing his place to Les Medley. Whilst with Spurs he received two Welsh caps to add to the two he had won with Swansea. In May 1949 he moved to Southampton as part of the deal that brought Alf Ramsey to Spurs. He served the Saints for over two years before ending his League career at Bristol City.

JONES, JOHN L. The first Tottenham Hotspur captain to receive the FA Cup, he was an inspirational figure and a great servant of the club. When he joined Spurs from Sheffield United in May 1897, he was already Wales's first choice left-half with nine caps to his credit. However, he spent most of his first season with the club at centre-half, although in those days centre-halves were not the defensive players expected in today's game. He was the brains of the team and one of the most skilful players of his day. When he played for Wales against Ireland on 19 February 1898 he became the first Spurs player to win international honours. Only two months after winning his twelfth cap as a Spurs player he left to join Watford. He did appear once more in Spurs' colours, returning in April 1907 to play for Spurs' 1901 FA Cup winning squad in a benefit match for trainer Sam Mountford. When his footballing days were over, he concentrated on coaching cricket, working in Leinster and South Africa.

JOYCE, BILL. Signed from Bolton Wanderers, Bill Joyce's scoring record was quite phenomenal. He scored on his debut and continued to do so in the two years he was with Spurs. In only 119 appearances, he scored 93 goals, including four hat-tricks, three fours and one five-goal haul. Yet despite this outstanding record, his only representative honour came when he represented the United League against the Thames and Medway League in 1898.

JOYCE, JOHN. A big strapping man, but an agile goalkeeper, John 'Tiny' Joyce is best remembered for his many years' service with Millwall. He first played for the Docklands club in 1900 and was first choice 'keeper until losing his place in October 1909. Spurs were finding life hard in their opening season in the First Division and Joyce was just the type of goalkeeper they needed, so his transfer was secured. In 1911 in a reserve match against Peterborough, 'Tiny' Joyce was reported as having punched the ball 76ft 2in. He also kicked a dead ball 94yd 2ft before the ball touched the ground and is the only goalkeeper to score for Spurs in a Football League game, netting against Bolton Wanderers in 1914. The arrival of Bill Jacques finished Joyce's career with Spurs and in 1916 he returned to Millwall.

JULL, JACK. One of the founders of Spurs, Jack Jull was also one of the finest players associated with the club in those early years. His first known appearance was in the first Spurs match to be reported in the local press when they entertained Brownlow Rovers and won 9–0. Rather oddly, he was mentioned in the match report but not included in the team line-up. He was the first Spurs player to win a representative honour when he played for Middlesex v Surrey on 18 February 1891. He later served on Spurs' committee for several years and in 1895 he was made the club president.

K

KINNEAR, JOE. Moving to London with his family when only seven, the Dublin-born full-back's big chance came when Phil Beal broke an arm and he stepped into the right-back position in time to join the 1967 FA Cup winning team. He gave a highly impressive Wembley performance and was the youngest player on the pitch. A quick, hard-tackling defender, he formed an excellent partnership with Cyril Knowles until his leg was broken in two places during a home match with Leeds in January 1969 and he was out of action for a year. He returned to play in the League Cup winning teams of 1971 and 1973 and won a winners' medal in the UEFA Cup of 1972. Both between and after these highs, he was kept out on merit by Ray Evans and in August 1975 he was transferred to Brighton and Hove Albion. He only played for one season at the Goldstone Ground before retiring, adding one more cap to the 24 he had won with Spurs. He later assisted his mentor, Dave Mackay, as coach at Doncaster Rovers before returning to London as a coach with Wimbledon. In January 1992, he rose to the post of manager following the dismissal of Peter Withe.

KIRKHAM, FRED. A well-known referee from Preston, having been in charge of the 1902 and 1906 FA Cup finals and many internationals, he was the club's surprise choice as manager following John Cameron's resignation in 1907. He was not a success as a manager and was unpopular with both players and fans. It came as no surprise when he resigned.

KIRWAN, JOHN. Born in Wicklow, Ireland, John Kirwan first came to England to play for Southport but was soon in demand and joined Everton as replacement for John Cameron who had moved to Spurs. When Frank Brettell resigned as Spurs' manager in February 1899, Cameron was appointed manager-secretary and Kirwan was one of the first players persuaded to join the club. One of the club's star performers, he helped Spurs win the Southern League championship and the FA Cup in 1901. A very fast outside-left, he formed a devastating partnership with David Copeland and though it was Sandy Brown who scored the goals, it was Kirwan and Copeland who provided the service for those strikes. At the final whistle in the FA Cup final replay victory over Sheffield United, Kirwan was first to the match ball and he kept it as a souvenir until he died. A total abstainer from drink and tobacco, he moved to Chelsea in 1905 where he won four more caps to add to the 12 he won with Spurs and another after joining Clyde for the 1908–09 season.

KLINSMANN, JÜRGEN. During the 1993–94 season, chairman Alan Sugar and manager Ossie Ardiles produced a masterstroke in securing the signature of German international Jürgen Klinsmann, whose reputation for diving had won him few friends in England. Born in Goppingen, in the Swabian heartland of south-west Germany, he scored 106 goals in one season as a nine-year-old, 16 goals in one game when he was 10 and 250 goals in four seasons in Germany as a teenager. At the age of 17 he signed professionally with Bundesliga Second Division side Stuttgart Kickers. He then rejected an approach by Kaiserslauten before controversially moving across the city for £250,000 to local rivals VFB Stuttgart. In 1987 he made his international debut for West Germany, the first of 68 caps, as a 23-year-old in a 1–1 draw with Brazil. The following year he finished the season as top scorer in the Bundesliga and crowned a brilliant campaign by being voted German player of the year. In 1989 he joined Inter Milan for £1.3 million. He achieved global stardom during Italia '90 when he scored three goals during the tournament to help Germany lift the trophy. In 1992 he turned down Real Madrid's approach and

Jürgen Klinsmann

joined AS Monaco in France. Having turned down offers from Aston Villa and Everton during the 1994 World Cup tournament, he arrived at White Hart Lane for £2 million. He opened his account on the first day of the season with the winner in a thrilling 4–3 win at Hillsborough over Sheffield Wednesday. He scored two more (one of them a spectacular overhead kick) in the next game, his home debut against Everton. Within five weeks of his first game for the club, the *Sunday Times* had christened him *Der Goalmeister* and the Spurs scoreboard flashed up 'Wunderbar' whenever he scored. It was the only word to describe the master class Klinsmann gave Watford in the art of striking. His hat-trick as Spurs won 6–3 in the Coca-Cola Cup in September included a fine goal with each of his feet and a classic header. At the end of a successful campaign personally, Klinsmann moved to Bayern Munich, with Alan Sugar alleging that he breached his contract by revealing confidential information to the German club in contract negotiations. It seemed as though Spurs had lost one of their favourite sons, such was his impact on English football in that one season that it rightly earned him the Football Writers' Association Footballer of the Year award.

KNOWLES, CYRIL. A great attacking full-back, his first professional club was Middlesbrough. After making his League debut in April 1963, he almost immediately caught the eye of Bill Nicholson and after only 39 appearances signed for Spurs for £45,000 in May 1964. The brother of Peter Knowles, who gave up his professional career with Wolves to become a Jehovah's Witness, he won six England Under-23 caps and four full caps in the late 1960s. He spent his initial North London season at right-back, moving to the left at the start of the 1965–66 season to replace Ron Henry. He was a member of Spurs' FA Cup winning team in 1967, played in the 1971 and 1973 League Cup final wins and the 1972 UEFA Cup success. He became a national cult figure when the pop song 'Nice One Cyril' became a national catchphrase. From December 1973 he was troubled by a serious knee injury and although he recovered to help save the club from relegation in 1975 with two goals in the final match with Leeds, the injury flared up the following season and he was forced into premature retirement. He went on to become a successful coach at Middlesbrough and manager of Darlington, Torquay United and Hartlepool. A brain illness forced him to quit Hartlepool in June 1991 and two months later he died at the early age of 47.

KYLE, PETER. A big bustling centre-forward, Peter Kyle scored in each of his first four competitive matches for Spurs. Clearly a valuable member of the team, he appeared to have a lengthy career with Tottenham in front of him, but along with Chris Carrick was guilty of a breach of the club's training rules in March 1906. Both players were suspended and neither of them played for Spurs' first team again. The following month Kyle signed for Woolwich Arsenal.

L

LACY, JOHN. An economics graduate, he made his League debut for Fulham in November 1972 and played for the Cottagers in the 1975 FA Cup final against West Ham United. Profiting from the vast experience of Alan Mullery and Bobby Moore, he soon attracted attention from the bigger clubs and signed for Spurs for £200,000 in July 1978. In fact, Lacy was the first man whose fee was fixed by a Football League tribunal. A tall, gangling centre-half, he worked hard on his skills in what was a difficult period for the newly promoted Spurs. However, as Graham Roberts and Paul Miller began to form a strong central defensive partnership, his long-term prospects were not good and in 1983 he moved to Crystal Palace.

LARGEST CROWD. It was on 5 March 1938 that White Hart Lane housed its largest crowd. The occasion was the FA Cup sixth round match against Sunderland. A staggering crowd of 75,038 saw Spurs lose 1–0 to the men from Roker Park.

LATE FINISHES. Spurs' final match of the season against Barnsley at White Hart Lane on 7 June 1947 is the latest date for the finish of any Tottenham season. During the war, many curious things occurred, among them the continuance of the 1940–41 season into June. Thus Spurs' last competitive match in that campaign was also on 7 June when goals from Ward (penalty) and Broadis gave them a 2–1 home win over Fulham.

LEAGUE CUP. See Football League Cup.

LEAGUE GOALS – MOST SCORED. Tottenham's highest goal tally in the Football League was during the 'double' winning season of 1960–61 when they scored 115 goals in winning the First Division championship.

LEAGUE GOALS – LEAST CONCEDED. During the 1919–20 season, Spurs conceded just 32 goals in 42 games when winning the Second Division championship.

LEAGUE GOALS – MOST INDIVIDUAL. Jimmy Greaves holds the Tottenham record for the most League goals in a season with 37 scored in the First Division during the 1962–63 season.

LEAGUE GOALS – CAREER HIGHEST. Jimmy Greaves holds the White Hart Lane record for the most League goals with a career total of 220 goals between 1961 and 1970.

LEAGUE VICTORY – HIGHEST. Tottenham's best League victory was the 9–0 win over Bristol Rovers at White Hart Lane on 22 October 1977. Colin Lee scored four of the goals and Ian Moores three. The other scorers were Glenn Hoddle and Peter Taylor. On 11 October 1958, Tottenham beat Everton 10–4 in the First Division. Bobby Smith scored four and Alfie Stokes two. The other goals came from John Ryden, Terry Medwin, Tommy Harmer and George Robb.

LEE, COLIN. Two days after joining Spurs in a £60,000 move from Torquay United in October 1977, Colin Lee grabbed the headlines with four debut goals in the 9–0 annihilation of Bristol Rovers. Though unable to maintain such a fairytale start, he played regularly during the season's successful campaign. In 1978–79 he showed great versatility when dropping back to centre-half or full-back but even though this made him an important squad member he was not really good enough for First Division football. Despite this, he moved to Chelsea for £200,000 and spent seven years with the Stamford Bridge club both as a striker and defender. In fact, it was as a full-back that he won a Second Division championship medal in 1984 but his Full Members' Cup medal came as a two-goal centre-forward! In July 1987 he joined Steve Perryman at Brentford before moving to Watford to take charge of their youth team. He later became manager at Vicarage Road before being replaced by Perryman!

LINDSAY, ALEX. He made several guest appearances for Spurs during the First World War and was signed in time for the resumption of League football. After making his debut against Coventry City in August 1919 he found that his first-team opportunities were few and far between as the club were blessed with players of the calibre of Banks and Cantrell. Gradually, Lindsay proved himself to be a more than competent performer in any of the forward positions. He was a most willing player who never gave up a lost cause and this accounted for many of the injuries which plagued him throughout his career. When Frank Osborne moved from the wing to centre-forward, he lost his place, but switched to left-half to replace Arthur Grimsdell who had broken his leg. In April 1930, he was released and moved to Thames before returning to Scotland with Dundee.

LINEKER, GARY. An outstanding talent of his generation, Gary Lineker started his career as a raw apprentice in 1977 at Leicester City and waited two years to make the grade in the first team. His 46 First Division goals in his final two seasons at Leicester made Lineker the hottest property in Britain. He was lured to the lofty surroundings of Goodison Park for £800,000 and immediately fitted into the team. He scored 30 League goals that season as Everton finished runners-up to Liverpool in both the League and FA Cup. Consolation was gained, however, from the fact that he was named the PFA Footballer of the Year and won the Golden Boot award as top scorer in Europe. There was also his contribution to England's World Cup campaign in Mexico. Against Poland, a first-half Lineker hat-trick blitzed away the opposition. As soon as the finals were over, he moved to Spain in a staggering £2.3 million move. With Barcelona he won a Spanish Cup and European Cup-winners' Cup medal. Terry Venables was Barcelona's master technician before he returned to England to

Gary Lineker

take over the managerial reins at Tottenham. It was therefore no surprise when Venables paid £1.2 million to bring Lineker to White Hart Lane in June 1989. With Gascoigne alongside him, he scored 24 goals to head the First Division charts in his first season with the club. Also, by this time Lineker was an established member of the England side. He was an integral member of the squad which played so well to reach the semi-finals of Italia '90. His qualities as a front runner spurred Tottenham to glory in their 1991 FA Cup campaign. Never booked in the whole of his career,

105

his services to football were rewarded in the 1992 New Year's Honours List with the OBE. Leading England to the 1992 European Championships, he announced the tournament would be his swansong as a top-flight professional. Determined to go out a winner, he left the England scene under a cloud as he was substituted by Graham Taylor in his final appearance against Sweden. However, his England record speaks for itself: 48 goals in 80 appearances – just one goal away from equalling Bobby Charlton's record. He announced he would be ending his career in the newly formed J League in Japan. He joined Nagoya Grampus Eight for £1.7 million in February 1993 and attained immediate superstar status. He announced his retirement from the game in September 1994 and now has a new career as a national radio and television personality.

LITTLEWOODS CUP. See Football League Cup.

LIVERMORE, DOUG. He started his career at Anfield, but after only 17 appearances moved to Norwich City, where he was an important member of the Canaries' promotion sides of 1971–72 and 1974–75. After joining Cardiff City, he helped the Welsh club to runners-up spot in the Third Division and when they won the Welsh Cup he played in the European competition. He was also coach at Swansea City in their glory days when they reached the First Division and was assistant to Mike England when the former Spurs centre-half was in charge of the Welsh national side. He arrived at White Hart Lane in 1984 to take charge of the reserves and in 1989 became assistant manager before becoming chief coach three years later. After Peter Shreeves departure from Tottenham in May 1992, he was placed in charge of team affairs with Ray Clemence. Spurs finished the season in eighth place. Now in his 12th year at Tottenham, he is the first team coach.

LONG SERVICE. The club's most illustrious personality is Bill Nicholson who joined Spurs as a ground staff boy in 1936. He made his League debut in 1938 as a full-back but his career was soon interrupted by the outbreak of war. After the war he returned to Spurs and established himself at right-half, but in 1954 joined Spurs' coaching staff, becoming assistant to boss Jimmy Anderson three years later. In October 1958, he was appointed manager. Under Nicholson, Spurs won the 'double' in 1960–61, the FA Cup again in 1962 and the European Cup-winners' Cup in 1963. He rebuilt the team to win the FA Cup in 1967 and then built a third team to win the Football League Cup in 1971 and 1973 and the UEFA Cup in 1972. After a poor start to the 1974–75 season, he resigned his post as manager after 16 seasons in charge. When Keith Burkinshaw was appointed manager in July 1976 he asked Nicholson to return as consultant. He did so and continued to serve the club in that capacity until 1991 when he was appointed club president.

LOWEST. The lowest number of goals scored by Tottenham Hotspur in a single Football League season is 38 in 1987–88. However, that was a 40-match programme; the club's lowest over a 42-match season is 45 in 1973–74. The club's lowest points record in the Football League occurred in 1914–15 when Spurs gained just 28 points and were relegated from the First Division.

LUDFORD, GEORGE. After playing with Tottenham juniors for two years he was sent to the Northfleet nursery and scored 101 goals as centre-forward in 1935–36. Such goalscoring form led to a move to the professional ranks at White Hart Lane. A prolific scorer for the reserves, he had few opportunities in the first team before the Second World War. It was only during the war that he had his chance but that was on the wing as the centre-forward role was filled by the great amateur Jack Gibbons. A loyal club man, he was happy to play in any position, but by the end of the war he had settled comfortably into the half-back role and had his best season in 1946–47, missing just one game. However, much of his later football was played with the reserve team until in 1954 he moved on to the coaching staff.

LUNN, TOMMY. Goalkeeper Tommy Lunn joined Spurs from Wolverhampton Wanderers in April 1910 as they struggled hard to avoid the drop after just one season in the First Division. He made his debut in the 2–0 win at Bolton, but the club still had to beat Chelsea in the last match of the season to avoid relegation. Lunn turned in a superb performance to deny the Stamford Bridge side. In November of that year he played for the Football League against the Southern League at White Hart Lane and was the club's regular goalkeeper for the next two seasons. In 1913 he took out a publican's licence which was frowned upon by the club's board and in breach of his contract – he was suspended.

LYMAN, COLIN. Rejected by West Bromwich Albion as being 'too frail' he joined Northampton Town, where he soon established himself as an out-and-out winger. Transferred to Spurs in October 1937, he played regularly in the last two full seasons before the Second World War. Unable to play for Spurs due to service demands, he guested for several other clubs and played in representative matches for the RAF and FA XI. When football resumed in 1946 he was allowed to move to Port Vale.

M

MABBUTT, GARY. One of a footballing family, his father Ray turned out for Bristol Rovers and Newport County and elder brother Kevin played for Bristol Rovers and Crystal Palace. He followed in his father's footsteps and signed for Bristol Rovers, making his Football League debut at Burnley in December 1978, whilst still an apprentice. During his four years at Eastville he showed great character as well as his great ability (he occupied every outfield position) when managing to keep his much discussed diabetes under control. He signed for Tottenham in August 1982 and made his League debut in midfield in the opening game of the 1982–83 season at Luton Town, although his first senior appearance came against Liverpool in the FA Charity Shield at Wembley. He eventually finished the season as the club's second highest League scorer. He made his first full England appearance against West Germany on 13 October 1982 in the right-back spot. He later played in a variety of positions for his country and his club. He led Spurs in the 1987 FA Cup final against Coventry City when, after putting his side 2–1 up in the first half, he deflected a Lloyd McGrath cross into his own goal. Four years later he ended with a winners' medal after leading Spurs to victory over Nottingham Forest. At one time he looked to be out of favour with the England management, but his consistency and reliability saw him recalled to the national side early in

Gary Mabbutt

the 1991–92 season for the qualifying games of the European Championships. He has never let his country down and has 16 caps to his name.

MACKAY, DAVE. Within months of making his debut for Hearts, Dave Mackay was the proud possessor of a League Cup winners' medal, won at the expense of Motherwell at a rain-swept Hampden Park in October 1954. Eighteen months later they lifted the Scottish Cup, but for Mackay and Hearts the best was yet to come. The League championship was captured in season 1957–58 and Mackay, who was now Hearts captain, was named Scotland's Player of the Year by *Sunday Mail* columnist Rex Kingsley, which was recognised to be the top individual award of the day. He won his first full cap for Scotland against Spain in Madrid in 1957. Although he went on to captain his country in only his third international, he had an erratic international career which brought him a paltry 22 caps in eight years! In March 1959, Hearts accepted an offer of £30,000 from Spurs, which Bill Nicholson was later to describe as his best day's work ever. Three

Dave Mackay

FA Cup wins, a League championship, including the coveted 'double' in 1961 and European Cup-winners' Cup triumph in nine unforgettable years at White Hart Lane provide the evidence of his greatness. Mackay also became the first Scotsman to represent the Football League in a representative match and was 'runner-up' to the legendary Stanley Matthews as Footballer of the Year in 1963. A twice fractured leg sidelined him for the best part of two years but the real tragedy was that by the time he had returned to full fitness, the great Tottenham side of the early '60s was no more. However, Mackay's will to win was as strong as ever and in 1967 one of Spurs' greatest-ever players helped them win the FA Cup for a third time in seven seasons. In 1968, when Brian Clough was looking for an on-field general to lead his promising Derby County side, he turned to the 33-year-old Tottenham warhorse. Twelve months later the title was won by seven points and Mackay, now playing as a sweeper, was named Footballer of the Year for 1969 alongside Manchester City's Tony Book. Since hanging up his boots, Dave Mackay managed Derby County to the First Division title and also had spells in charge of Swindon

Town, Nottingham Forest, Walsall, Doncaster Rovers and Birmingham City, as well as coaching in the Middle East.

McALLISTER, DON. After helping Bolton Wanderers win the Third Division title in 1972–73, he earned a reputation as one of the best central defenders in the Second Division. Determined and uncompromising, McAllister was signed for £80,000 in February 1975 to strengthen a Spurs side that was fighting against the threat of relegation. Initially slotting in as a midfield ball-winner, he went on to give five years of solid service in the back four, performing at various times in every outfield position. Some of his best displays came in a central role alongside Steve Perryman as Spurs won promotion from the Second Division at the first attempt. After two consistent seasons in the top flight, he suffered a bad injury in 1980–81 and he joined Charlton Athletic. With his contract up at the end of the season, Spurs said they had written to him with a new offer. The blond Lancastrian claimed not to have received any letter from the club and he was therefore entitled to a free transfer.

McCLELLAN, SID. A prolific scorer for Chelmsford City in the Southern League, he first came to Spurs' attention in January 1948 when he scored a hat-trick in a friendly against Tottenham reserves. A deadly finisher, with a tremendous burst of speed, he stayed at White Hart Lane for seven years, but was never classed as a regular. However, McClellan does have the distinction of having scored more goals for the club in a single match than any other player. He scored nine times when Spurs beat the Saskatchewan FA XI 18–1 in May 1952 during their tour of North America.

McCORMICK, JIMMY. The speedy winger attracted the attention of his home-town club, Rotherham, but it was Chesterfield who offered him professional terms. Following injuries to Les Howe and Taffy O'Callaghan, he signed for Spurs in March 1933 to help their push for promotion. Following their success, he missed only two games as the club finished third in the First Division in 1933–34. Even though Spurs were relegated the following season, it was McCormick's intricate wing play that brought the crowds to White Hart Lane. An injury early in 1937–38 virtually finished his Tottenham career, though during the war years he guested for many other clubs.

McDONALD, BOB. A strong, hard-tackling full-back, he was signed from Inverness Caledonians in August 1919. His chances of establishing himself at right-back were blocked by the outstanding performances of Tommy Clay, but the experiment of playing him at left-back was a huge success and he finished the season with an FA Cup winners' medal.

McELHANEY, RICHARD. He made his debut in the club's first Southern League match at Sheppey United in September 1896 and went on to be an almost ever-present that season. His outstanding wing play was responsible for many of the goals scored by Bob Clements. There is no doubt that the dashing McElhaney would have been retained for the following season but after an 'act of insubordination' in April 1897 he was suspended. Released at the end of the season he joined Swindon and, later, Brentford.

McKAY, KENNY. A hard-working inside-forward with an eye for goal, Kenny McKay scored on his first appearance for Spurs, in a friendly against Gainsborough Trinity, the United League, Thames and Medway League and FA Cup. It was only in the Southern League that he failed to mark his debut in the competition with a goal. The 1898–99 season proved to be his only one with Spurs, the decision to release him being rather mystifying.

McNAB, NEIL. He joined Spurs in February 1974 for £40,000 – a raw 16-year-old who had played Scottish First Division football with Morton a year earlier! A hard-working midfield player it took him until 1977–78 to establish a place in the Spurs team, but he was an ever-present in the Second Division promotion campaign. With the arrival of Ardiles and Villa, he lost his place and in November 1978 he joined Bolton Wanderers for £250,000. He then moved around, playing for Brighton, Leeds United and Portsmouth (both on loan) and then Manchester City. The Maine Road fans saw the best of his performances as he helped City win promotion to the First Division in 1989 and was voted Player of the Year. He moved to Tranmere and appeared at Wembley in two Leyland Daf finals. Huddersfield, Ayr, Darlington, Derry City and Witton Albion were his next ports of call before he returned to Maine Road as youth team coach.

McNAUGHT, JAMES. The Dumbarton-born player was close to international honours and played for the Anglo-Scots against the Home Scots in the 1899 international trial. However, a month earlier he played for an England XI against a Scotland XI in a match to raise money for the Players Union! A member of the Spurs team that won the Southern League in 1900, he missed out on the FA Cup success of 1901, collecting an injury against Preston North End in the first round.

McWILLIAM, PETER. Peter McWilliam excelled as a player and as a manager. He played in Newcastle United's great sides between 1905 and 1910, winning three Football League championship medals and one FA Cup winners' medal. A quiet man, he was extremely popular with the players and though his side was relegated in 1914–15, he helped the club win the Second Division title in 1919–20, the FA Cup in 1921 and to their highest-ever First Division position of second in 1921–22. Approached by Middlesbrough to become their manager, he asked Spurs for a rise and being refused he handed in his notice. Spurs later regretted his loss and tried to entice him back, but did not succeed until 1938. He was to remain at White Hart Lane for little more than a year before war was declared. He returned to the north-east, but by the time the hostilities ended he decided he was too old for football management and retired.

MANAGERS. In a 98-year history, Tottenham Hotspur Football Club have had only 19 managers. They have been as follows:
1898–1899 Frank Brettell
1899–1907 John Cameron
1907–1908 Fred Kirkham
1912–1927 Peter McWilliam
1927–1929 Billy Minter
1929–1935 Percy Smith
1935–1938 Jack Tresadern
1938–1939 Peter McWilliam
1946–1949 Joe Hulme
1949–1955 Arthur Rowe

1955–1958 Jimmy Anderson
1958–1974 Bill Nicholson
1974–1976 Terry Neill
1976–1984 Keith Burkinshaw
1986–1987 David Pleat
1987–1991 Terry Venables
1991–1992 Peter Shreeves
1993–1994 Ossie Ardiles
1994–   Gerry Francis

MARATHON MATCHES. Spurs have been involved in a number of cup games that have gone to three matches. These were Bolton Wanderers (FA Cup fifth round 1934–35); West Ham United (FA Cup fourth round 1938–39); Birmingham City (FA Cup sixth round 1952–53); Middlesbrough (Football League Cup third round 1972–73); Portsmouth (Football League Cup fourth round 1985–86) and Arsenal (Football League Cup semi-final 1986–87), though this was a two-legged match. The FA Cup tie against Birmingham City in 1952–53 attracted 162,692 spectators over the three matches.

MARCHI, TONY. London-born of an Italian father, he was a schoolboy prodigy who appeared in the Spurs' reserve team when only 15 and then, as an England Youth international, made his League debut as a 17-year-old against Grimsby in 1950. He eventually settled into the wing-half position and in the mid-'50s inherited the great Ron Burgess's shirt. An ever-present for the 1954–55 and 1955–56 seasons, he was appointed captain and played for England 'B'. However, Italian club Lanerossi made a £42,000 offer, which was far too good for either the club or Marchi to refuse and so Spurs reluctantly agreed to let him leave. after a season with Lanerossi, he played for Torino and Juventus before Spurs re-signed him for £20,000 in July 1959. With Dave Mackay now in Marchi's old left-half berth and playing well alongside Danny Blanchflower, he was unable to get back into the team. Good enough to walk into most other First Division teams, his Italian experience was crucial in 1962–63 when he played as an extra defender in the European Cup-winners' Cup competition. In June 1965 he left for the player-manager's job at Cambridge City before having a year in charge of Northampton Town.

MARKSMEN, LEAGUE. Spurs' top League goalscorer is Jimmy Greaves who struck 220 League goals during his nine years at White Hart Lane. Only eight players have hit more than 100 League goals for the club.

1. Jimmy Greaves	220
2. Bobby Smith	176
3. Cliff Jones	135
4. George Hunt	125
5. Martin Chivers	118
6. Len Duquemin	114
7. Les Bennett	104
8. Jimmy Dimmock	100
9. Billy Minter	95
10. Alan Gilzean	93

MARKSMEN, OVERALL. Thirteen players have hit a century of goals for Spurs. The club's top marksman is Jimmy Greaves. The Century Club consists of:

1. Jimmy Greaves	266
2. Bobby Smith	208
3. Martin Chivers	174
4. Cliff Jones	159
5. George Hunt	138
6. Alan Gilzean	133
7. Len Duquemin	131
8. Les Bennett	118
9. Jimmy Dimmock	112
10. Glenn Hoddle	110
11. Bert Bliss	104
12. John Morrison	104
13. Billy Minter	101

MEADS, THOMAS. He was a member of League champions Huddersfield Town's 1926–27 side who were striving to win the title for a fourth successive year. They finished second as they did the following season and so Meads, finding himself out of favour, moved to Reading. He signed for Spurs in May 1929 and made his debut in the opening match of the following season when Spurs played Bradford Park Avenue. A combative left-half, he made 196 senior appearances over the next five seasons, helping Spurs win promotion in 1932–33. He was not retained at the end of the 1934–35 season and joined Notts County.

MEDLEY, LES. A local schoolboy star, he signed as an amateur in the summer of 1935, before turning professional with Spurs in February 1939. He played regularly in the first season of wartime football before service in the Royal Air Force took him to Canada, where he met his wife. He returned to Tottenham for the latter war years, but his wife became homesick and in 1946 he emigrated to Canada. In January 1948 he returned to both Spurs and England, although it took him time to re-establish himself in the side. When he did, he became one of the most important players in the 'push and run' team that won the Second and First Division titles in successive seasons. In fact, this fast and direct winger was top goalscorer when they won the Second Division championship and reached double figures when they won the League championship the following season. He made his England debut against Wales in November 1950. This was the first of six caps and he was never on the losing side. He retired at the end of the 1952–53 season to return to Canada.

MEDWIN, TERRY. A Welsh international signed from Swansea Town for £18,000 in May 1956, he had proved himself a versatile forward, occupying all the front line positions with the Swans. During his time at Vetch Field he played in 148 League games, scoring 59 goals. Making his Spurs debut on the opening day of the 1956–57 season, he scored twice as Preston North End were beaten 4–1. Best remembered at White Hart Lane as a fast, dangerous winger, he won 29 caps, all but the first three while with Spurs. He was occasionally played at centre-forward, the role in which he struck four times in the 6–0 home thrashing of Leicester City in April 1959. A Tottenham regular for four seasons, he was unfortunate to lose his place to the aggressive Dyson in the 1960–62 'double' season, although he played 15 League and FA Cup games as deputy for either Jones or Dyson. He gained some consolation in 1962 when he was a member of the Spurs side that retained the FA Cup. A broken leg on the 1963 tour of South Africa brought premature retirement. He later returned to the professional game by coaching at Fulham, and then served his home-town club Swansea as assistant manager to John Toshack.

MIDDLEMISS, BERT. Until a few weeks before his move to Spurs, Bert Middlemiss had been an amateur with Stalybridge but because he had signed professional forms for Stockport, it was to the Edgeley Park side that Spurs paid the transfer fee. A fast, raiding winger always eager to cut inside and shoot at goal, he made his debut against Brentford in November 1907 and played regularly until the First World War, making more League appearances for Spurs before the hostilities than any other player. Playing in four international trials, he was always on the verge of an international cap, yet the only representative honour he won was in April 1910 when he played for the Football League against the Southern League, Unavailable for Spurs during the war, he guested for Birmingham and Coventry but was past his best when normal football resumed and was released to join Queen's Park Rangers for their first season in the Football League.

MILK CUP. See Football League Cup.

MILLER, LES. Les Miller was signed from the French club Sochaux in 1936. This followed his scoring of 60 goals in the previous season and he thus became the first player to join a Football League club who had played professionally in France. A fast, well-built and intelligent winger, he played regularly for most of his first season at White Hart Lane but over the next two years had to vie with Colin Lyman for a position.

MILLER, PAUL. He spent a season with Skeid in the Norwegian League before establishing himself in the Spurs first team. He helped Spurs win the FA Cup in 1981 and 1982, reach the Football League Cup final in 1982 and win the UEFA Cup in 1984 when he headed the crucial away goal in the first leg in Anderlecht. However, his position in the team always seemed under threat, both with the signings of Lacy, Price and Stevens and the emergence of Culverhouse, O'Reilly and Webster. His unseating came in 1986 when David Pleat signed Richard Gough and paired him in the middle of defence with Gary Mabbutt. He left White Hart Lane for Charlton in February 1987, later playing for Watford, Bournemouth, Brentford and Swansea.

MILLIKEN, JIMMY. Spurs' regular inside-right during the

1896–97 season, he made a goalscoring debut in the club's 3–3 draw with Sheppey United in their first Southern League match. After playing in the majority of matches that season he was suspended for an 'act of insubordination'. However, he did play in one more match for the club, but that was in the Wellingborough Charity Cup. He was not retained and returned to Scotland to play for Clyde.

MIMMS, BOBBY. Starting his career with Halifax Town, he moved to Rotherham United without ever making the Shaymen's first team. At Millmoor he became the first choice 'keeper from March 1984 and was an ever-present the following season when he won two England Under-21 caps, both times as substitute. In the summer of 1985 he moved to Everton as cover for Neville Southall and after a spell on loan to Notts County, returned to Goodison Park, where his big chance came in April 1986. With Southall injured, he stood in and ended the season with an FA Cup runners-up medal. However, Southall was always number one and on recovering to full fitness he resumed his place. Mimms was loaned out to Sunderland, Blackburn Rovers and Manchester City before Spurs signed him for £375,000. Sadly, his reign at White Hart Lane lasted less than one year as he lost his place to Norwegian international Erik Thorstvedt. After two years of understudying the Norwegian 'keeper and a short period on loan to Aberdeen, he was sold to Blackburn Rovers for £250,000, whom he helped gain promotion to the top flight via a Wembley play-off final in 1992.

MINTER, BILLY. A well-built inside-forward, Billy Minter scored his fair share of goals each season. After helping Spurs win promotion from the Second Division in 1908–09 he was top scorer for the next three seasons. He was absent for most of the First World War due to military service, but in 1919–20 he was back to help lift the club into the First Division. At the end of that season he announced his retirement and became the club trainer, although he still turned out in the occasional friendly match. When Peter McWilliam resigned as manager he was asked to replace him. He was in charge for almost three years and in his first full season the club was relegated. He took the failure to get Spurs back into the First Division so personally that it made him ill and in November 1929 he resigned. His service to the club was well appreciated, so much so that he was not allowed to leave and was made assistant secretary, a position he filled until his death.

MOORES, IAN. A gangling, sometimes awkward-looking centre-forward, he joined Spurs for £75,000 from Stoke City in August 1976 on the recommendation of England trainer Les Cocker, who had been taken with his performances as an Under-23 international. He scored in his first two games for the club, but then the goals and his confidence dried up as Spurs were relegated to Division Two. The high point of his White Hart Lane career came in October 1977, when he contributed a hat-trick towards the 9–0 demolition of Bristol Rovers. A year later he moved to Orient whom he served for four years before joining Bolton Wanderers.

MONTGOMERY, JOCK. When he signed professional forms for Spurs in January 1896, Jock Montgomery may well have become the first professional player at the club. He was pitched straight into the first team and went on to give the club first-class service at left-back for over two years. His only goal for the club came in the Boxing Day clash of 1896 when Spurs beat Vampires 4–0 in a friendly, Montgomery playing at centre-forward. Moving to Notts County, Jock spent 13 years as first-choice left-back before finishing his career with Glossop North End in 1914–15.

MORGAN, ROGER. He was signed for £110,000 from Queen's Park Rangers to provide a supply of crosses from the flanks for Jimmy Greaves and Alan Gilzean which had been missing since the release of both Cliff Jones and Jimmy Robertson. In his first match, at Loftus Road curiously, he set up a goal for Greaves and on his home debut against Wolves, he scored in a 1–1 draw. He won an England Under-23 cap in April 1970 and looked a good long-term prospect until he was injured early the following season. It was the first of several knee injuries that sadly forced the happy-go-lucky Londoner into premature retirement in the summer of 1973. He retained his sporting connection by becoming a Football in the Community Officer with West Ham United.

MORRIS, TOM. A powerful, workmanlike half-back, he did much to establish Spurs as one of the major clubs in Southern football during the earliest part of the century. He had made his reputation with Grantham Rovers and Gainsborough Trinity before joining Spurs in 1899. After making his debut against Queen's Park Rangers he went on to appear in more Southern League matches than any other Spurs player. An important member of the side that won the Southern League in 1899–1900, he played in the first senior match at White Hart Lane and was an ever-present in the FA Cup winning team of 1901. Morris was also the only member of that great team still with Spurs when the club entered the Football League in 1908–09. He played for the South against the North in international trial matches, but never won the full international cap he so richly deserved. After 13 years of outstanding service he retired from playing in the summer of 1912 to take up a position on the White Hart Lane ground staff. He remained with the club until his death 30 years later.

MORRISON, JOHNNY. Johnny Morrison marked his first-team debut against Chesterfield on 1 April 1933 with a goal, but failed to make the League side the following season as George Hunt continued to lead the attack. Despite scoring 36 goals in 28 reserve outings, he played in only three games in the 1934–35 season and it wasn't until Jack Tresadern took over the manager's chair from Percy Smith that he got his chance. There is no denying that Morrison was an opportunistic goalscorer. His remarkable goalscoring record of 90 goals in 134 League appearances speaks for itself. He was still Spurs' first choice centre-forward on the outbreak of the Second World War but when he returned to the club in December 1945 he played only one game before announcing his retirement.

MOST MATCHES. Spurs played their most number of matches, 66, in 1971–72 season. This comprised 42 League games, five FA Cup games, seven Football League Cup games and 12 UEFA Cup games when they won the trophy.

MULLERY, ALAN. Born in Notting Hill, he signed as a professional for Fulham in December 1958 and helped them to win promotion to the First Division in his first season. After more than 200 appearances for the Cottagers he moved to Spurs for £72,500 in March 1964. Two months later he played for the Football League against the Italian League and after one more outing with the Football League won his first full cap against Holland in December that year. Restricted at international level by the performances of Nobby Stiles, he did not win his second cap until May 1967, four days after winning an FA Cup winners' medal against Chelsea. After that he became an England regular winning 33 more caps. In 1968 he became club captain and led the club to victory in the 1971 League Cup final. However, in October that year he began to suffer from a deep-seated pelvic strain which put him out of action for six months. On recovery, he went on loan to Fulham, but after a month was recalled owing to a lengthy injury list at Spurs. Leading the club into their UEFA Cup semi-final with AC Milan, he clinched the tie with a brilliant 20-yard volley at San Siro before going on to secure the trophy with a header – he knocked himself out in the process – in the second leg of the final against Wolves. He returned to Fulham in the 1972 close season for a fee of £65,000 and in 1975 won an FA Cup runners-up medal, was elected Footballer of the Year and awarded the MBE. When he retired he moved into management at Brighton and led them from the Third to the First Division before moving to Charlton. He spent only a year with the Valiants before managing Crystal Palace and Queen's Park Rangers for two years each and then finishing career with another spell at Brighton.

MURPHY, PETER. Top scorer for Coventry City in 1949–50, Spurs signed him for £18,500 to strengthen a squad that had just won the Second Division title. He scored on his debut as Spurs won 4–1 at Bolton, provided strong opposition to Les Bennett and ended the season with a Football League championship medal. Unable to command a regular place, Spurs agreed to transfer him to Birmingham City, where he scored over 125 goals in more than 250 appearances to help City win the Second Division championship in 1955 and reach the FA Cup final 12 months later. It was Murphy who was involved in the accident in that 1956 FA Cup final which resulted in Bert Trautmann breaking his neck. He retired from first-class football in 1960 and ended his playing career with a year at Rugby Town before having a spell on Coventry's coaching staff.

NAYIM. The multi-talented Moroccan-born Spaniard was given his chance in Barcelona's senior team by Terry Venables. He then suffered a serious knee ligament injury but when he was first to return, the Spanish club's new manager, Johann Cruyff, who had replaced Venables, made it clear he was surplus to requirements. Venables persuaded Nayim to join Spurs on loan for 18 months but such was his impact at White Hart Lane that Tottenham opted to make the transfer permanent, securing his services for a bargain £300,000 as a make-weight in the Gary Lineker deal. Thereafter he tended to drift in and out of the Spurs side, sometimes through injury and sometimes through inconsistency. He proved his value when replacing the injured Paul Gascoigne in the 1991 FA Cup final victory over Nottingham Forest, but more widely appreciated was his hat-trick in Spurs' FA Cup sixth round victory at Manchester City in 1993. However, a few weeks later he joined Real Zaragoza for £500,000 and in 1995 lobbed David Seaman in the Arsenal goal from fully 45 yards to take the European Cup-winners' Cup to Spain.

NAYLOR, TERRY. A one-time porter at Smithfield Market he joined Spurs in July 1969 and stayed for more than 11 years. Originally a defensive midfield player, the club's array of talent in that position meant that he had few opportunities and so when he did get the chance to deputise it was usually as a central defender, notably covering for Phil Beal. However, when Cyril Knowles injured his knee in December 1973, he was given his chance at left-back. Making the position his own, he played in both legs of the 1974 UEFA Cup final. Following the departure of Kinnear and Evans, he showed his versatility by playing in the number two shirt. Even though Spurs were relegated in 1976–77, he stayed with the club and helped them to promotion the following season. A wholehearted defender who always gave the impression he would run until he dropped for the sake of Tottenham Hotspur, he moved across London to Charlton Athletic in November 1980. Playing in a pre-season friendly against West Ham in August 1982, he broke his leg and this eventually forced his retirement from the game.

NEIGHBOUR, JIMMY. A strong-running and tricky winger, he had to compete with Jimmy Pearce and Roger Morgan at first, but his chance came in 1970–71 and after only a few first-team games he won a League Cup winners' medal against Aston Villa. His progress was halted by the signing of Ralph Coates but in the mid-'70s he became a regular choice under Terry Neill. However, in September 1976, with Keith Burkinshaw in charge, Spurs signed Peter Taylor and Neighbour was immediately transferred to Norwich City for £75,000, against whom he'd made his last appearance for Spurs a few days earlier. After three years at Carrow Road, he moved to West Ham United and helped them reach the 1980 FA Cup final, although he did not play in the final itself. He was in the Hammers' losing League Cup final squad and remained at Upton Park for four years until his retirement in 1983. In October 1990 he returned to West Ham as their Youth Development Officer.

NEILL, TERRY. Born in Belfast, he joined Arsenal in 1959 from Bangor and served as their centre-half and captain for 11 years until moving to Hull City as player-manager. He made his international debut for Northern Ireland against Italy in Bologna in April 1961 and went on to play 59 games for his country. When he joined Hull in June 1970, he was only 28 and chairman of the PFA. He also took on the responsibility of being player-manager of Northern Ireland at this time until March 1975, when pressures at White Hart Lane forced him to quit the job. Appointed Spurs manager in September 1974, he took over a side in decline and unable to compete in the top end of the transfer market – he tried to sign Johann Cruyff and Charlie George – he struggled. He had appointed Keith Burkinshaw as his coach in 1975 and it was Burkinshaw who got most of the credit for the club's improvement when they had a good run to avoid relegation at the end of the 1974–75 season. following a dispute over players' bonuses, he resigned and almost immediately took on the manager's job at Highbury.

NEUTRAL GROUNDS. Whilst White Hart Lane has been used as a neutral ground for FA Cup matches on a number of occasions, Spurs themselves have had to replay on a neutral ground a number of times; the most important being the FA Cup final of 1901. Spurs had drawn 2–2 with Sheffield United at the Crystal Palace before the game was replayed at Burnden Park, the home of Bolton Wanderers. The FA's original choice had been Goodison Park, but Liverpool had a home game on the same day. However, after conceding the first goal, Spurs took command and won 3–1. The club's FA Cup semi-finals were of course played on neutral grounds. Of their 14 appearances in this stage of the competition, seven have been at Villa Park, five at Hillsborough and two at Wembley when they met local rivals Arsenal. Tottenham's FA Cup finals at Crystal Palace, Stamford Bridge and Wembley also qualify for inclusion.

NEWBIGGING, WILLIE. Spurs' regular centre-forward throughout the 1896–97 season as the club made its debut in the Southern League, he was a regular scorer in friendly matches and scored a hat-trick in a 4–0 win over Casuals. However, he found it difficult to find the net in competitive matches and was released at the end of the season.

NICE ONE, CYRIL. Catchphrase that swept the United Kingdom in the 1970s. Popularised by a television advert for Wonderloaf in 1972, the phrase became particularly relevant to football around 1973, when it was chanted by fans of Tottenham Hotspur to the side's left-back Cyril Knowles – subsequently immortalised in a pop song released by the 'Cockerel Chorus':

Nice one, Cyril
Nice one, son
Nice one, Cyril
Let's have another one.

NICHOLLS, JOE. A giant, reliable goalkeeper, Joe Nicholls signed for Spurs after giving a wonderful display in the Army Services Bulldog Challenge Cup. Though he made his first-team debut at Anfield in April 1927, he had to wait until the start of the 1932–33 season before making the spot his own, as he served a lengthy apprenticeship as Cyril Spiers' understudy. An ever-present in 1933–34 when Spurs finished third in the First Division, he played for the Rest v England in the international trial of March 1934. Extremely popular with the crowd, his form suffered at the start of the 1935–36 season and by the end of it he had joined Bristol Rovers.

NICHOLSON, BILL. One of the greatest managers of British soccer, he was the architect of one of the finest club sides the world has ever seen. In the early 1960s his Spurs team played exhilarating, flowing football. They won the League and FA Cup double in 1960–61, the first club to do so in the 20th century. This remarkable triumph was followed by a steady stream of Cup successes as Spurs went marching on. He

"TURF" CIGARETTES

W. E. NICHOLSON
TOTTENHAM H.

joined the club as a ground staff boy in March 1936 and was farmed out to Spurs' nursery club, Northfleet, where he developed over the next two years. In 1938 he signed professional forms and made his debut at left-back at Blackburn some two months later. His career was soon interrupted by the war and when he returned to White Hart Lane after the hostilities, he turned out at centre-half, before establishing himself at right-half. He played in Arthur Rowe's side which won the Second Division championship in 1949–50 and the League title the season after. His one and only appearance for England against Portugal at Goodison Park saw him score from long range with his first kick of the game after a matter of seconds. He made 345 League and Cup appearances for Spurs before retiring in 1954 to take up a coaching post within the club. In August 1957 he became assistant manager and then in October 1958 took over from Jimmy Anderson as manager. His first game in charge saw Spurs beat Everton 10–4. He began to develop sides with great style and allowed his players to show off their skills and entertain the crowds. Success came on the field and Spurs' double-winning side of 1960–61 was one of the greatest-ever club line-ups in English soccer. The following season they won the FA Cup again and in 1963 they won their first European trophy when they beat Atletico Madrid 5–1 in the European Cup-winners' Cup final. He was in the process of rebuilding the Spurs side when they won the FA Cup again in 1967. They also won the League Cup in 1971 and 1973 and the UEFA Cup in 1972. After a poor start to the 1975–75 season, Nicholson surprised most people by resigning as manager after 16 years in charge. The players and directors tried to persuade him to change his mind but to no avail. He took a deserved rest from the game before returning to work as consultant to West Ham United, but within months he was back at White Hart Lane as chief adviser and scout. He was awarded the OBE in 1975, a testimonial game at Spurs in August 1983 and the PFA Merit Award in 1984. In May 1991 he was appointed Spurs president.

NICKNAMES. Tottenham's nickname is usually 'the Spurs'. Also many players in the club's history have been fondly known by their nicknames. They include:
Eddie Baily (1945–56) 'The Cheeky Chappie'
Tommy Harmer (1949–60) 'The Charmer'
John White (1959–64) 'The Ghost'
George Hunt (1930–37) 'The Chesterfield Tough'
Len Duquemin (1953–60) 'The Duke'

NON-LEAGUE. Since the formation of the Football League in 1898, only one non-League team has won the FA Cup: Tottenham Hotspur, then of the Southern League, beat First Division Sheffield United 3–1 at Burnden Park, Bolton, in 1901 after a 2–2 draw at Crystal Palace. Spurs have played non-League opposition in the FA Cup on a number of occasions, the most recent being Marlow on 2 January 1993 when they won 5–1 in a game played at White Hart Lane. On 13 January 1913, they met Worksop Town of the Midland League in the first round of the FA Cup. Worksop had surrendered their home draw and played away at White Hart Lane. With four minutes of the match remaining and the game goalless, Worksop hit the crossbar and the ball scrambled clear. Spurs won the replay 9–0!

NORMAN, MAURICE. Making his name as an uncompromising centre-half in the Spurs 'double' team, he arrived at White Hart Lane in November 1955 from Norwich City for £18,000. A giant of a player, whose shock of wavy black hair made him appear even taller than 6ft 1in, he was a commanding figure in the air and an awesome tackler. Norfolk-born, he had played only 35 League games for the Canaries when he joined Spurs in a deal engineered by Jimmy Anderson which saw Johnny Gavin go from Tottenham to Carrow Road. He won his first England Under-23 cap against Scotland in February 1956 and two more the following season, but it wasn't until the autumn of 1957 that he could call the central position his own. He had quite a long wait for full international honours and though he was a member of England's squad for the 1958 World Cup, he had to wait until 1962 for his chance. After that he went on to win 23 caps for his country. Apart from his 1960–61 club honours, he won an FA Cup winners' medal the next season and was a member of the 1963 European Cup-winners' Cup winning team. His career suffered a rather abrupt end in 1965 when his left leg was broken in five places in a home friendly against a Hungarian XI. Despite a two-year fight for fitness, during which his shinbone had to be reset, he was forced to retire.

NORTH AMERICA. Immediately after the end of the 1951–52 season in which Spurs finished as runners-up to Manchester United, they accepted an offer to tour North America. All ten games, including two against Manchester United, were won and included Spurs' highest scoring result in any first-team match – an 18–1 victory over the Saskatchewan FA XI in Saskatoon on 26 May 1952. Sid McClellan scored nine goals in that game. On that tour Spurs scored 85 goals and conceded just six!

NORTHUMBERLAND PARK. Tottenham moved to their first enclosed ground at Northumberland Park in 1888. This was a playing field behind the Northumberland Arms public house on Trulock Road, on the other side of the railway line from Tottenham Marshes and only a hundred yards from the present ground. Rent was fixed at £17 a year and the club's first game was in September of that year, a reserve match against Stratford St Johns. The first stand was not built until 1894 and it was not for another year that professionalism was adopted. The stand cannot have been terribly substantial because soon after it blew down in a gale. Northumberland Park was closed down once, in 1898, when Spurs' fans invaded the pitch and assaulted three Luton Town players. The ground's highest recorded attendance was 14,000 for a match against Woolwich Arsenal in April 1899. During that game the roof of a refreshment stall, on which many spectators were sitting, collapsed causing several minor injuries.

NUMBERING. In 1933 Tottenham Hotspur proposed that players should be numbered in Football League matches, but it was defeated at the annual general meeting. In the Cup final that year, both teams were numbered for the first time but from 1–22. Numbering of players in the Football League became official from the start of the 1939–40 season.

O

O'CALLAGHAN, TAFFY. The star of Tottenham's forward line throughout the late 1920s and early 1930s, he was working in the pits when invited to join the club's ground staff in 1925. A clever player who packed a good shot in either foot, he scored plenty of goals for the club. After making his debut against Everton in February 1927, replacing the injured Jimmy Seed, he soon became a great favourite with the White Hart Lane crowd. In fact, he did so well that Seed was unable to regain his place and eventually left the club to join Sheffield Wednesday. O'Callaghan continued to go from strength to strength and made his first appearance for Wales against Northern Ireland in May 1929. He won 11 full caps in his time with Spurs and scored twice when Wales beat Scotland 5–2 in October 1932. Having helped the club to promotion in 1932–33, he was surprisingly transferred to Leicester City in March 1935 when Spurs were struggling to avoid relegation. He won a Second Division championship medal with the Filbert Street side in 1936–37 before

PLAYER'S CIGARETTES.

E. O'CALLAGHAN.
TOTTENHAM HOTSPUR.

moving to Fulham early next season. He played with the Cottagers until 1945–46, then worked on the training staff until his death.

O'HAGAN, CHARLIE. A neat, skilful inside-forward, most of Charlie O'Hagan's appearances for Spurs were as stand-in for David Copeland, but when he did play, he complemented fellow Irishman John Kirwan well. Signed from Everton, he was by no means a regular for Spurs but won five international caps for Ireland during his stay at White Hart Lane. In May 1906 he was released and joined Middlesbrough, but after a few months moved on to Aberdeen, where he won a further six caps. After the war he was appointed manager of Norwich City for their Football League debut but within six months he had resigned.

OLDEST PLAYER. The oldest player to line up in a Tottenham first team is Jimmy Cantrell. Jimmy was born on 7 May 1882 and was 40 years 349 days when he played his last game for the club against Birmingham City (home 2–0) on 21 April 1923.

OSBORNE, FRANK. The son of an army colonel, Frank Osborne was born in Wynberg, South Africa, and returned with his family to England in 1911. He joined amateur club Bromley in 1919 and within two years had signed for Fulham. In January 1924 Spurs paid £1,500 for his signature and over the next seven seasons he made 220 senior appearances, scoring 82 goals. Had he played regularly at centre-forward, he would have scored more goals, but his slight build was considered more suitable to the wing. He had won two caps whilst with Fulham and to  emphasise his versatility, Osborne won two more caps as a Spurs player, at centre-forward and on the wing. It was at centre-forward that he scored a hat-trick against Belgium in 1926. In 1931 he moved to Southampton, where he played for two years before retiring. He later returned to London to manage Fulham and in his first season led them to the Second Division title.

OSGOOD, KEITH. An England schoolboy and youth international, he was just three days past his 19th birthday when he made his debut at Newcastle in May 1974. There followed a few outings at the start of the next season but he then returned to the reserves until February 1975 when Mike England left the club. A stylish defender who was capable of cracking home free-kicks from anything up to 35 yards, he impressed immediately with his speed, agility and composure and looked set for a fine future. However, when his form wavered in December 1977, he was dropped and reacted by demanding a transfer. The request was granted by manager Burkinshaw and he moved to Coventry City for £125,000, after which he played for Derby County, Orient and Cambridge United without being able to fulfil all that early potential.

OVERSEAS PLAYERS. Probably the first foreigner to play in the Football League was Max Seeburg. Although born in Leipzig he was brought up in the Tottenham area. In 1978 Spurs added a new dimension to their game when Argentinians Osvaldo Ardiles and Ricardo Villa joined the club fresh from their country's World Cup triumph. Since then the club has boasted a number of continental players. These have included Dutchman Johnny Metgod, Belgian Nico Claesen, Spain's Nayim, Norway's Erik Thorstvedt and Iceland's Gudni Bergsson. In 1994 Rumania's Popescu and Dumitrescu joined the club along with German international Jürgen Klinsmann. Spurs have also had John Chiedozie, a Nigerian international, on their books. Other players with foreign-sounding surnames include Milija Aleksic, Harry Erentz and Tony Marchi – all born in the British Isles!

OWN GOALS. Playing for Spurs against Burnley at White Hart Lane on 5 October 1974, Mike England and John Pratt both put through their own goal during the first half. After the interval both scored for their own side. Gary Mabbutt also scored for both sides when Spurs played Coventry City in the 1987 FA Cup final at Wembley.

P

PARKS, TONY. The young goalkeeper carved a niche for himself in the club's glorious history in the second leg of the 1984 UEFA Cup final against Anderlecht. When the final finished 2–2 on aggregate and extra time failed to produce a winner, the game went to a penalty shoot-out. With Spurs 4–3 ahead, he dived to his right, clawed the ball away and then celebrated ecstatically with his team-mates. It was his second save in that shoot-out and brought the UEFA Cup to Tottenham. He was only playing as stand-in for the injured Ray Clemence, a situation that he found himself in for all his career at White Hart Lane. Indeed, he had appeared in only 18 League games before the first leg of that UEFA final. His career was resurrected again in 1987–88 when Clemence was injured and he enjoyed a prolonged spell of First Division football. However, after 19 consecutive games he was dropped in favour of new-signing Bobby Mimms. He was allowed to leave Spurs in July 1988 and joined former White Hart Lane favourite Steve Perryman at Brentford. He later played for Queen's Park Rangers, Fulham, Southend United, West Ham United and Falkirk.

PARROT. At the end of the 1908–09 season Spurs travelled to South America for matches in Argentina and Uruguay. One of the souvenirs that the club acquired was a parrot. On the voyage home, a fancy dress contest was held and due to the efforts of Charlie Roberts it was won by two Spurs players dressed as Robinson Crusoe and Man Friday. One of the props was the ship's parrot and to mark the event it was presented to Roberts. It remained a Spurs mascot until 1919.

PAYNE, ERNIE. Throughout the 1892–93 season, Ernie Payne was on Fulham's books but only played twice for the first team. Accepting an invitation on 21 October 1893 to play for Spurs in a reserve match, he went to Fulham to collect his kit, only to find it had disappeared. Arriving at Northumberland Park without any equipment, shorts and a shirt were found for him but no boots were suitable. So Spurs loaned Payne ten shillings to go and buy a pair. When Fulham heard of this they complained to the London FA that Spurs were guilty of 'poaching' and 'professionalism'. Acquitted of the poaching charge, Spurs were found guilty of misconduct in offering Ernie Payne an 'inducement' to play for them. The manner in which Spurs were treated led to Spurs adopting professionalism two years later. Payne took up the offer of paid football until forced to retire due to a knee injury.

PEARCE, JIMMY. A very skilful player, able to play as a central striker, winger or in midfield, he was at his best as an orthodox winger. An England schoolboy international, he had the unenviable task of following Cliff Jones, Terry Medwin and Jimmy Robertson. He made his debut during Spurs' summer tour of Greece and Cyprus in 1968 and his League debut against Arsenal at the start of the following season. He never managed to become completely established but was unfortunate to be omitted from the 1971 League Cup final team and named substitute, especially after he had scored in the semi-final. However, he at least had the consolation of playing in the Spurs team that won the trophy in 1973. It seemed that at last his confidence was matching his ability when he suffered persistent knee pain that was linked to a rare bone condition and he never played top-level soccer again.

PENALTIES. Gary Lineker is one of only two players (John Aldridge is the other) to miss a penalty in an FA Cup final. This he did in the 1991 final against Nottingham Forest which Spurs won 2–1 after extra-time. Danny Blanchflower (v Burnley 1962) and Glenn Hoddle (v Queen's Park Rangers 1982) successfully converted theirs.

PENALTY SHOOT-OUT. Spurs have been involved in the most memorable penalty shoot-outs. Facing Anderlecht in the 1984 UEFA Cup final, Spurs drew the first leg in Belgium 1–1, but then had to rely on a Graham Roberts goal six minutes from the end of normal time at White Hart Lane to take the game into extra time. With no further scoring, the result hinged on a penalty shoot-out. After Anderlecht's first kick was saved, Spurs went into a 4–3 lead. Then came drama as Danny Thomas's penalty was saved – if he had scored the trophy was won! Then Tony Parks, who was only playing because of injury to Ray Clemence, pulled off a superb save to give Spurs the UEFA Cup.

PERRYMAN, STEVE. The most consistent and loyal player Spurs have ever had, he holds the record of having appeared in more matches for the club than anyone else. An England youth cap, he was already a first-team player when he played in Spurs' 1970 FA

Steve Perryman

Youth Cup winning team. Originally a midfield player, he dropped back into the back four in 1977 and later played as full-back. He played in over 1,000 first-team games in his 17 years at White Hart Lane, such was his consistency. He won more Spurs honours than any other player – League Cup winner (1971 and 1973), UEFA Cup winner (1972), captain of two FA Cup final teams (1981 and 1982) and captain of the 1984 UEFA Cup winners, although he had to miss the second leg through suspension. He won 17 England Under-23 caps, but only one full cap, as substitute against Iceland in June 1982. That season he was voted Football Writers' Association Player of the Year. He was awarded a testimonial in April 1979 and the MBE in the Queen's 1986 Birthday Honours List. A truly great professional and loyal club man, he finally left Spurs in March 1986 to join Oxford United for £50,000. He later moved to Brentford as player-assistant manager, was promoted to manager and led the Bees to the sixth round of the FA Cup and Third Division play-offs in 1989. He surprisingly resigned in August 1990, but three months later took over as manager of Watford, following the dismissal of his former Spurs team-mate Colin Lee. He steered them clear of relegation in 1990–91 when the drop looked inevitable, but in July 1993 he returned to White Hart Lane as Ardiles' assistant.

PETERS, MARTIN. An England youth cap, he made his League debut for West Ham United in April 1962 and by November of that year was playing for the England Under-23 team against Belgium. He was a member of the Hammers' European Cup-winners' Cup winning team of 1965 and League Cup final team of 1966. He won his first full cap against Yugoslavia in May 1966, just in time for the World Cup. With his West Ham colleagues Bobby Moore and Geoff Hurst, he helped England lift the Jules Rimet trophy, scoring one of the goals that beat West Germany in the final. In March 1970 he became Britain's first £200,000 footballer in the transaction that took Jimmy Greaves to Upton Park. Though he scored with a header on his Spurs debut, a home defeat by Coventry, he took time to settle. His first representative honour with Spurs was a substitute for the Football League against the Scottish League and his first cap with Spurs against Wales in April 1970. In total he won 34 caps whilst with Spurs. He was a member of the teams that won the League Cup in 1971 and

1973 and the UEFA Cup in 1972. He was made Spurs captain following the departure of Alan Mullery. A midfield player with the knack of scoring goals from blind-side runs, he was allowed to move to Norwich City in March 1975 for £50,000. The fee proved a bargain as he went on to play over 200 League games for the Canaries before moving to Sheffield United as player-coach. His great contribution to the game was recognised with the award of an MBE in 1978. A player whom Alf Ramsey had once described as ten years ahead of his time, he did enough to suggest that he was a player who could have appeared at the highest level in any era.

PITCH. The White Hart Lane pitch measures 110 yards x 73 yards.

PLASTIC. There have been four Football League clubs that replaced their normal grass playing pitches with artificial surfaces at one stage or another. Queen's Park Rangers were the first in 1981, but the Loftus Road plastic was discarded in 1988 in favour of a return to turf. Luton Town, Oldham Athletic and Preston North End followed. Spurs have never played on the Deepdale plastic and won 4–2 in the FA Cup third round tie at Oldham's Boundary Park in January 1988. Though Spurs' record on the Loftus Road and Kenilworth Road plastic is not a good one, it is probably no worse than that of most clubs. They did manage three consecutive goalless draws at Luton, whilst in 1985–86 they won 5–2 at Queen's Park Rangers with goals from Falco (2), C. Allen (2) and Hoddle.

PLEAT, DAVID. A highly respected and innovative manager, David Pleat started his career with Nottingham Forest before being transferred to Luton Town, then Shrewsbury, Exeter and Peterborough United. In 1971 he joined Nuneaton Borough as player-manager before returning to Luton Town as coach the following year. In 1978 he was promoted to manager and over the next eight years was responsible for establishing the Hatters as a First Division club renowned for attractive, attacking play. They only just avoided the drop in 1982–83 by winning their last game against Manchester City, with a goal four minutes from time by Raddi Antic, thus sending down the opposition instead. Many probably remember Pleat galloping across the pitch to hug his players in delight. He joined Spurs in May 1986 and the following season lifted the club to third place in the First Division and took them to the FA Cup final and a League Cup semi-final, both of which they lost after holding the upper hand. He was responsible for the introduction of the style of play which saw a five-man midfield in support of a lone front runner. However, early in the 1987–88 season he resigned after lurid newspaper allegations about his private life. He was not out of the game for long and accepted the manager's job at Leicester City. He lost his job when the Filberts were nearly relegated in 1991 and returned to Kenilworth Road before becoming manager of Sheffield Wednesday.

POINTS. Under the three points for a win system which was introduced in 1981–82, Spurs' best points tally was the 77 points in 1984–85 when the club finished third in the First Division. However, the club's best points haul under the old two points for a win system was 70 points in 1919–20 when they won the Second Division championship. Spurs' worst record under either system was the meagre 28 points secured in 1914–15 when they were relegated.

POYNTON, CECIL. Signed from the Welsh League club Ton Pentre, Cecil Poynton gave Spurs over 50 years' service as a player, trainer and physiotherapist. Playing at full-back, he was a member of the FA touring team to Australia in 1925 and represented the Professionals against the Amateurs in the FA Charity Shield match in November of that year. Though he continued to appear in the first team for the next six years, he never really made the position his own. After studying physiotherapy, he became Spurs assistant trainer in 1946 and in 1972, when over 70, became the club's physiotherapist.

PRATT, JOHN. A non-stop midfield player, he worked his way through the junior and reserve ranks to make his debut against Arsenal in March 1969. He had to wait until the 1971–72 season for a settled stint, coming in for the sidelined Alan Mullery. Playing alongside Perryman and Peters he prompted attacks and won a UEFA Cup-winners' medal that season. The following campaign he helped Spurs reach Wembley, but after only 20 minutes of the League Cup final against Norwich he was forced to leave the field injured. For the rest of the '70s his name was rarely absent from the teamsheet and in 1977–78 he was an ever-present as Spurs gained promotion from the Second Division at the first attempt. Often made the scapegoat and a target of a section on The Shelf, he won them over with his industrious displays – 24,000 attending his testimonial game with Arsenal in 1978. He remained with Spurs until May 1980 when he opted for a fresh challenge across the Atlantic with Portland Timbers. After three years he returned to White Hart Lane as youth team coach and assistant manager until both he and Peter Shreeves were dismissed in April 1986.

PRATT, TOM. It was at Preston North End that big Tom Pratt first showed his prowess. A tough centre-forward, his signing for Spurs in April 1899 caused quite a stir. He spent only 12 months at White Hart Lane but made his mark, scoring the goals that won Spurs their only Southern League championship and helped them finish runners-up in the Southern District Combination. However, he could not settle in London and returned north to Preston.

PREMIER LEAGUE. Teddy Sheringham was the Premier League's top scorer in its inaugural season 1992–93 with 22 goals, all but one of them scored when with Spurs. It was always destined to be a season of consolidation and development for a predominantly inexperienced squad. The 1993–94 campaign was not exactly a vintage one for Tottenham as they narrowly avoided relegation. The following season saw the club get themselves in with a realistic chance of a place in Europe but with only two wins from the final ten games the chance was lost.

PRICE, PAUL. Paul Price twice broke his leg whilst playing for Luton Town reserves, but battled back and developed into a cultured central defender. He helped the Hatters gain promotion to the First Division in 1973–74 and by the time of his £250,000 move to Spurs in June 1981 he had a total of 11 full caps for Wales, whom he qualified for through his father who was born in Merthyr Vale. He suffered an early blow in his second match at home to West Ham when an injury left him sidelined for several months. On his return to fitness, he found it difficult to replace regular central defenders Miller and Roberts. However, he still represented his country and won a further 14 caps as a Spurs player. He played in the Spurs teams that won the 1982 FA Cup but lost out in the Milk Cup final. A combination of injuries and the form of Miller and Roberts limited his opportunities and in the summer of 1984 he was allowed to move to Minnesota Kicks. He later returned to these shores to play for Swansea City and Peterborough United.

PROMOTION. Spurs have been promoted on five occasions and always from the Second Division to the First. They were first promoted in 1909 at the end of their first season in the Football League when they finished runners-up to Bolton Wanderers. They were promoted a second time in 1920 after winning the Second Division championship, finishing six points clear of Huddersfield Town. In 1933 they were promoted for a third time, finishing one point behind Stoke City. They were promoted again in 1950 after winning the Second Division championship and finishing nine points ahead of Sheffield Wednesday. They were last promoted in 1978 when they drew 0–0 at Southampton to clinch the point needed to go up. Spurs are one of only a handful of clubs who have won the Second and First Division championships in consecutive years, winning the Second Division title in 1950 and the First Division a year later.

PUSH AND RUN. A style of tactical play in which attacks were mounted on bursts of speed and short accurate passes. The technique was developed by Arthur Rowe when he became Tottenham manager in 1949 and it brought the club championship titles in 1950 and 1951.

Q

QUAGMIRE. When Spurs played Wolves at Stamford Bridge in the FA Cup final of 1921, they made light of a cloudburst during the game which turned the pitch into a quagmire. Spurs' best player on the day was centre-half Charlie Walters, who dominated the Wolves forwards and even found time to prompt his attack from deep lying positions. The only goal of the game was scored by Jimmy Dimmock in the 54th minute. Taking a pass from Bert Bliss he lost the ball to Woodward, but the Wolves defender took too long to clear the ball and Dimmock regained possession and advanced to shoot past the goalkeeper from 15 yards with an oblique shot which went in at the far post.

QUICKEST GOAL. The club's records do not include precise goal times since 1882 and so it is an impossible task to state accurately the club's quickest goalscorer. Whilst there have obviously been quicker goals, Clive Allen's near-post header gave Spurs a second-minute lead in the 1987 FA Cup final at Wembley.

R

RAMSEY, ALF. Alf Ramsey was a fine international full-back who helped Spurs to successive titles culminating in the League championship in 1951. He also became one of the most famous managers of all time, taking England to their World Cup triumph over West Germany in 1966, after earlier guiding Ipswich Town from the Third Division to the League title in little over five years. As a player he was a strong, polished and distinguished defender who joined Portsmouth as an amateur in 1942 and a year later moved to The Dell. He made his England debut in a 6–0 victory over Switzerland at Highbury in December 1948, before going on to make 28 consecutive appearances for his country. In all he won 32 caps for England and represented the Football League on five occasions. In May 1949 he moved to Tottenham Hotspur for a record fee for a full-back of £21,000. Virtually an ever-present in the teams that won the Second Division and Football League titles in 1950 and 1951, he was very accurate with penalties and free-kicks and developed into a great reader of the game. In May 1955, after 250 League and Cup games for Spurs, he retired. In August 1955 he became manager of Ipswich Town and led them to the Third Division (South) title in 1956–57, the Second Division championship in 1960–61 and then the First Division title in 1961–62. In January 1963 he was appointed as the first full-time manager of England. His greatest triumph came in 1966 when England, playing on home territory, took the World Cup for the first and only time. In May 1974, after England had failed to qualify for the finals of that year's World Cup competition, he was sacked. Under Ramsey England lost only 17 out of 113 games and had won 69 of these. In September 1977, at the age of 57, Sir Alf was appointed manager of Birmingham City. He held office for only six months, before being forced to relinquish the position due to ill health.

RANCE, CHARLIE. A goal-scoring member of Clapton's Amateur Cup winning team of 1907, Charlie Rance gave Spurs great service between 1911 and 1921. A hard-working and determined centre-half, he always tried to be creative with his distribution from defence. During the First World War Rance made more appearances for Spurs than any other player and when the game returned at League level in 1919–20 he was still first-choice centre-half as Spurs won the Second Division championship. The signing of Charlie Walters put Rance's place in jeopardy and he moved to Derby County but within 18 months he returned to London to join Queen's Park Rangers.

RAPID SCORING. On 7 February 1993 Tottenham Hotspur were trailing 1–0 to Southampton in a Premier League match at White Hart Lane when they scored four goals, courtesy of Sheringham (2), Anderton and Barmby in 4 minutes 44 seconds timed at: 54 minutes 45 seconds; 56 minutes 17 seconds; 57 minutes and 59 minutes 29 seconds. Spurs won 4–2.

RECEIPTS. The club's record receipts are £336,702 for the First Division match against Manchester United on 28 September 1991. The British record is £2,016,000 paid by the 80,000 fans who watched the 1991 FA Cup final between Spurs and Nottingham Forest. Including television fees that figure is increased to nearly £3 million.

RECORDS. Spurs have beaten plenty of records over the years but have also produced a couple of records that are among the most successful football discs. 'Ossie's Dream (Spurs are on their way to Wembley)' was released in May 1981. It was in the charts for eight weeks and reached number five. They followed that up in May

1993 with 'Tottenham, Tottenham', that was in the charts for seven weeks but only went as high as number 19.

RE-ELECTION. Re-election is determined by votes cast by League clubs and associate members. A variety of voting systems has been used over the years. On occasions, the re-election voting has resulted in a tie between two clubs. The closest voting came in 1908 when Tottenham Hotspur and Lincoln City tied on the first three ballots. The matter went to the League management committee who voted five to three in favour of Tottenham.

REID, JIMMY. Signed from Watford in 1906, he scored a hat-trick on his initial debut for the club in a 6–4 win over London Caledonians in a friendly match. Making his Southern League debut some nine days later against Norwich City, he finished the season as top scorer with 18 goals. In 1907–08 he was one of six players Spurs tried out in the troublesome inside-left position, but none was successful and exactly two years after joining the club he left to move to Southern League rivals Reading.

RELEGATION. Spurs have been relegated on only four occasions. Their first taste came in 1914–15, but fortunately they were promoted in the next possible season, 1919–20. They were next relegated in 1927–28 when they amassed 38 points. This is the record number of points obtained by a relegated club under the two-points-for-a-win system. The club were relegated for a third time in 1934–35. Finishing bottom of the table, they went through a stage of playing 16 League games without a win. Spurs' fourth and final experience of relegation came in 1976–77. Almost three decades of great success had come to an end, but as in their first experience of relegation they were promoted after just one season out of the top flight.

REYNOLDS, RON. He made his Football League debut for Aldershot in 1946 but it was not a happy occasion as Bournemouth put seven goals past him! However, he was a more than proficient goalkeeper and went on to make over 100 League appearances for the Shots. He joined Spurs in July 1950 as cover for Ted Ditchburn but had to wait until March 1954 before making his Spurs debut at home to Sunderland. A very capable deputy, there were times when Reynolds kept his place on merit but Ditchburn always seemed to bounce back. Reynolds, who wore contact lenses, moved to Southampton on transfer deadline day 1960 for £10,000. He helped the Saints win the Third Division before a shoulder injury forced him to retire.

RIPSHER, JOHN. A pillar of the local community, John Ripsher was warden of Tottenham YMCA and took bible classes at the nearby parish church of All Hallows. In August 1883 he was elected President of Hotspurs FC, a position he held throughout the club's formative years. He came to the club's rescue on two occasions. The first of these was when the club were asked to leave the YMCA following a council member being struck by a soot-covered ball. Ripsher found the club a new home at Dorset Villas, Northumberland Park, but after some of the members were caught playing cards in a church pew they were also asked to vacate Dorset Villas. Again Ripsher came to the rescue and found them new quarters at Red House in Tottenham High Road. It was 1894 when Ripsher resigned as president, though he remained with the club as patron.

ROBB, GEORGE. England amateur international George Robb first signed amateur forms for Spurs in 1944. Not offered professional terms by Spurs, he became a schoolmaster but continued to play for Finchley, where he won 18 amateur caps in his nine years with them. He made his debut on Christmas Day 1951 and scored in a 3–0 victory over Charlton Athletic. Signing professional forms in June 1953, he played under three managers in a period of under-achievement by the club. In 1953–54, his first full season, he scored 16 times in 37 matches and won one full international cap. Unfortunately, it came in the memorable match against the majestic Hungarian side when England were crushed 6–3. Although he did not win any more full honours, he did play in three 'B' internationals. Continuing to perform reliably at club level, he enjoyed an active FA Cup campaign in 1956. After scoring three times in the early rounds, he was about to push the ball into an empty net for the equaliser in the semi-final against Manchester City when Bert Trautmann appeared to grab his legs – amazingly no penalty was given! He suffered a serious knee injury during 1957–58 which forced him into retirement in May

1960 and a full-time return to the classroom.

ROBERTS, GRAHAM. Having been rejected by Southampton, Bournemouth and Portsmouth, he played part-time for Weymouth whilst working as a fitter's mate in a shipyard. By the end of the 1979–80 season Spurs and West Bromwich Albion wanted to buy him, Roberts chose Tottenham, signing for £35,000 in May 1980, a record fee for a non-League player. Within 12 months, having established himself at centre-half, he was helping his new club to victory over Manchester City in the 100th FA Cup final. A hard-tackling, aggressive player, he was a folk hero with the Spurs crowd. The following season he earned a second FA Cup winners' medal with his long attacking run early in the replay bringing about the penalty from which Glenn Hoddle scored the winning goal. He won his first England cap in May 1983 when he appeared against Northern Ireland. In his time at White Hart Lane he won six full caps and one 'B' cap. In 1984 he captained Spurs in Steve Perryman's absence and led the side to victory over Anderlecht in the UEFA Cup final, scoring the crucial late equalising goal that took the final into extra-time and the ensuing penalty shoot-out. In December 1986 soon after David Pleat's arrival he was transferred to Glasgow Rangers for £450,000. In his first season he helped them win the Scottish Premier Division title and in 1988, the Skol Cup. He later moved to Chelsea before joining West Bromwich Albion in November 1990. He later managed non-League Enfield.

ROBERTSON, JIMMY. Best remembered at White Hart Lane as a flying right-winger supplying the crosses for Greaves and Gilzean, he joined Spurs from St Mirren for £25,000 in March 1964. He played for Scotland against Wales soon after he came south and won four Under-23 caps. Though never a prolific scorer he loved to cut inside and try a shot at goal. His finest performance for Spurs came in the 1967 FA Cup final against Chelsea when he scored the opening goal to put the club on the way to their fifth FA Cup victory. In October 1968 he was allowed to leave and moved to Arsenal in a £55,000 deal which saw David Jenkins travel in the opposite direction. It was perhaps not one of Bill Nicholson's better decisions. He stayed at Highbury for two years before giving useful service to Ipswich and Stoke and then winding down his career with stints at Walsall and Crewe.

ROSENTHAL, RONNIE. An Israeli international, he arrived at Anfield in March 1990 following experience with Maccabi Tel Aviv and Belgian clubs FC Bruges and Standard Liege. He initially went to Liverpool on an extended loan and was immediately effective, adding an extra dimension to the attack just when it was most needed. He made his Football League debut against Southampton on 31 March 1990 and two weeks later when deputising for the injured Ian Rush at Charlton Athletic scored a remarkable hat-trick. Following this his appearances became limited and in January 1994 he moved to Spurs for a fee of £250,000. He responded with a vital equaliser in a 1–1 draw with Aston Villa as Spurs turned their season round with two draws and a win in late March. In 1994–95 he came on as substitute in Spurs' fifth round FA Cup replay at Southampton when they were 2–0 down. He scored a scintillating hat-trick in a 6–2 extra-time victory.

ROTTERDAM. Scene of Tottenham's first European triumph. It was here on 15 May 1963 that Spurs beat Atletico Madrid 5–1. The scorers were Terry Dyson (2), Jimmy Greaves (2) and John White as Spurs became the first British club to win a major European trophy.

ROWE, ARTHUR. Arthur Rowe will remain an important part of English soccer history as the man who invented a style of play called the 'push and run' method which helped Spurs win the League title for the first time in their history. He was a brilliant tactician who would have had even more success in soccer management but for a number of bouts of ill health. During his playing career he would have gained more than one cap for England had he not suffered so many injuries. Born a stone's throw away from White Hart Lane, he made his League debut against Burnley in October 1931 and quickly established himself as first choice centre-half. Spurs finished runners-up in Division Two in 1932–33 and third in the First Division the following season. The highlight of his playing career was his England cap which came against France at White Hart Lane in December 1933. Shortly afterwards he sustained an injury which restricted his appearance for the club and after 201 League and Cup appearances he was

Arthur Rowe (right) with trainer Cecil Poynton

released in May 1939 having failed to recover fully from cartilage problems. He was appointed by the Hungarian government as a national coach but this ended with the outbreak of war and he returned to England to serve in the army. On demobilisation he became secretary-manager of Chelmsford City until May 1949 when he became manager of Tottenham Hotspur. The celebrated 'push and run' style was to take Spurs to successive titles in Divisions Two and One in seasons 1949–50 and 1950–51. This entailed a player quickly passing the ball along the ground and running into open space to receive the return pass, or decoy an opposing player. In April 1955 his health broke down and his assistant, Jimmy Anderson, became caretaker manager until Rowe's contract expired some nine months later. Initially Rowe retired, but his love of the game brought him back. In 1957 he accepted a coaching post at West Bromwich Albion and in 1958 he became assistant manager at Crystal Palace. After guiding Palace to promotion to Division Three, he again suffered from ill health and resigned. From May to December 1971 he was secretary of the short-lived Football Hall of Fame – this was a museum about the game. In January 1972, at the age of 66, Arthur Rowe became general adviser at Orient and he remained there until

June 1978 when he joined Millwall as a consultant.

RUDDOCK, NEIL. After playing one game in Charlton Athletic's youth team, he joined Millwall where he became an England youth international. He transferred to Spurs a month after signing professional forms, without a single League appearances at The Den, and made his Football League debut at White Hart Lane against Charlton on 18 April 1987. At the end of the following season he returned to Millwall for £300,000, six times the original amount. Unable to gain a regular place with the Lions he moved yet again, this time to Southampton, for £250,000. He was an important member of the Saints team, helping them fight off relegation for two seasons. However, he marred some of his fine displays with major lapses of discipline – in 1991–92 he was sent off twice and booked in every other game up to Christmas. In another bizarre twist to his career, he returned to White Hart Lane for £750,000 in May 1992 as Spurs sought a dominant centre-half around which to rebuild the team. One of the few players ever released and then re-signed by Spurs he joined Liverpool for £2.5 million in July 1993.

RUMBELOWS CUP. See Football League Cup.

RUNNERS-UP. Spurs have been First Division runners-up on four occasions. When they achieved this position for the first time in 1921–22, it was the highest ever achieved by a London club.

RYDEN, JOHN. The blond Scot developed into a powerful-tackling centre-half with Accrington Stanley and when signed by Spurs for £8,400 in November 1955 was regarded as the best in his position in the Third Division (North). After waiting five months for his debut, playing when Harry Clarke was injured, he scored at Preston in a 3-3 draw. With Clarke's career drawing to an end, Ryden was given his first settled run in 1956–57 before making way for the younger Maurice Norman. He reclaimed the number five shirt at the start of the 1957–58 season and was made captain following the departure of Tony Marchi. That season he played his finest football, making 35 League appearances including a spell at left-half. He remained at White Hart Lane until June 1961 when he joined Watford.

S

SAMWAYS, VINNY. Winning England youth caps before he made his Football League debut against Nottingham Forest in May 1987, he made great strides the following season to become a valuable member of the first-team squad. However, there were occasions when he found it hard to hold down a permanent place and it may be that he did not benefit from the midfield presence of new arrival Paul Gascoigne. In 1990–91, with Gascoigne often absent through injury, he was given the chance to exert some influence on the Tottenham midfield and earned his first club honour when he won an FA Cup winners' medal following Spurs' 2–1 victory over Nottingham Forest. With his own maturity growing and Gascoigne's impending departure for Lazio, he looked set to make the creative midfield position his own, but it wasn't to be, for in July 1994 he signed for Everton for £2 million.

SARGENT, FRED. A fine attacking winger, Fred Sargent was playing for Tufnell Park when Spurs spotted his potential. Sent to Northfleet for three months to develop, he then joined the White Hart Lane staff and made his debut against Derby County in September 1934. It was another three years though before he made the outside-right spot his own. He enjoyed nothing better than taking on his full-back and beating him for pace. He also scored his fair share of goals, but was not always available for selection. In February 1940 he broke his leg at Chelsea and in football terms had a poor time during the war years. At the end of the war his contract was cancelled by mutual consent and he joined Arthur Rowe at Chelmsford City. Sadly, within two years Fred Sargent was dead, just 36 years of age.

SAUL, FRANK. Hailing from Canvey Island, he played in the Football Combination when 15 and made his League debut when just turned 17. An England youth international, he deputised for the injured Bobby Smith during the 'double' season and scored three goals in six games. He appeared in early European games and netted twice in the away leg of the clash with Feyenoord. Whilst versatile, being able to play on either wing as well as centre-forward, he lacked consistency and failed to take his chance when Smith left for Brighton in 1964, although he did score a hat-trick in a 4–1 win over Burnley. His best season at White Hart Lane was 1965–66 when he stood in for Jimmy Greaves, who was laid low with hepatitis. He finished the season playing for Young England against England in the annual eve of FA Cup final match. The following season he scored the winning goals in both the FA Cup semi-final against Nottingham Forest and the final itself against Chelsea. Strong and eager and with no shortage of skill he eventually moved to Southampton as part of the record deal which brought Martin Chivers to Spurs. Two years at the Dell were followed by two more at Queen's Park Rangers and then five at Millwall where he ended his senior career.

SCREEN SPORT SUPER CUP. Sometimes known simply as the Super Cup. The cup was contested just once, during the 1985–86 season between the six teams who could have qualified for Europe. Spurs reached the two-legged semi-final stage, but went down to Everton 3–1 after extra-time after a goalless first leg at White Hart Lane.

SCORES – HIGHEST. Tottenham's highest score in any first-team match was their 18–1 win over the Saskatchewan FA XI on their North American tour of 1952. The club's best victory in the FA Cup is 13–2 over Crewe Alexandra in a fourth round replay on 3 February 1960. In the Football League, Everton were beaten 10–4 in a First Division match in 1958–59 and Bristol Rovers were beaten 9–0 in a Division Two encounter in 1977–78.

SECOND DIVISION. Spurs have had five spells in the Second Division. The first was their initial League season 1908–09. At the end of that season they finished second to Bolton Wanderers. They survived six seasons in the top flight before sliding back into the Second Division. But again it was just for one season, 1919–20, as at the end of the campaign they topped the table. Their third experience of Second Division football came in 1928–29 and lasted for five seasons before they won promotion. Unfortunately their stay in the First Division lasted only two seasons before they were relegated in 1934–35. It was 1949–50 before they returned to the top flight, Spurs finishing nine points clear of Sheffield Wednesday their nearest rivals. Spurs' last taste of the lower division was in 1977–78, but again it lasted only one season.

SEDGLEY, STEVE. A Spurs fan as a boy, he trained at the club in his schoolboy days and even appeared in the junior team, but he was not offered a chance with Spurs and joined Coventry City. After making his League debut against Arsenal in August 1986, he had three years of steady progress before finding himself the subject of a £750,000 offer from Spurs. Joining the club in July 1989, he immediately fitted into the middle of the back four alongside Gary Mabbutt. He won his first international honour as a Spurs player in September 1989 playing for the Under-21s against Sweden. He remained first choice for Spurs until the end of the 1990–91 season and pocketed an FA Cup winners' medal in the 2–1 defeat of Nottingham Forest. A disappointing display at Southampton on the opening day of the following season signalled a period of uncertainty for him and in 1992–93,. with Neil Ruddock and Jason Cundy on the scene, the future did not look good for him. However, Sedgley is a true competitor and he fought back to be an ever-present in 1993–94. Surprisingly, in June 1994, he was allowed to leave White Hart Lane and joined Ipswich Town for £1 million.

SEED, JIMMY. One of the most important and influential players of the 1920s, Jimmy Seed had excellent vision and a good shot. Born at Blackhill, County Durham, he signed for Sunderland just before the First World War. After the hostilities had ended he returned to Roker Park but found himself released. The north-east club doubted that Seed could recover from the effects of a slight gas attack suffered on active service. He was signed by Mid-Rhondda and after a few games showed the gas had left no ill effects. Spurs signed Seed in February 1920. During his seven months with the Welsh side he had set them on the way to winning the Second Division of the Southern League, the Welsh League and the Welsh Cup. He was a fine tactician and masterminded the club's FA Cup success of 1921, scoring a hat-trick against Bradford City. He was rewarded with a first England cap against Belgium in May that year and won four more in his time with Spurs. An automatic choice for the club, he suffered a bad ankle injury that allowed Taffy O'Callaghan into the team. His transfer to Sheffield Wednesday in August 1927 is one of the worst deals in the history of the club. Spurs went down to the Second Division and Seed captained Wednesday to two League titles. He retired at the end of the 1930–31 season and moved into management with Clapton Orient. He later managed Charlton Athletic, taking them from the Third to the First Division and to two FA Cup finals, one victorious.

SEMI-FINALS. Up to the end of the 1995–96 season, Tottenham Hotspur had been involved in 14 FA Cup semi-finals and eight Football League Cup semi-finals.

SHELF. The Shelf is the favourite gathering place for home supporters. It is a standing area below the balcony of the East Stand. When the future of the Shelf was threatened by the club, fans united in opposing any change and won a reprieve for their popular haunt.

SHERINGHAM, TEDDY. After graduating through Millwall's junior sides, he made his Football League debut at the Den against Brentford in January 1984. Following a spell on loan at Aldershot, he returned to Millwall and in 1986–87 he was an ever-present scoring 18 goals. Following two seasons in the top flight, Millwall found themselves back in the Second Division for the 1990–91 season. Although the Lions failed at the play-off stage, Teddy Sheringham had a magnificent season, scoring 33 League

Teddy Sheringham

goals, including four in a 4–1 win over Plymouth Argyle and three further hat-tricks. He ended the season as the highest goalscorer in the club's history. In the summer of 1991 he joined Nottingham Forest for £2 million and though he ended the campaign as the club's top scorer with 12 Football League goals and nine Cup goals, he was not an unqualified success. After two games of the 1992–93 season he returned to London when joining Spurs for £2.1 million. He ended the season with 29 goals and won the Premier League Golden Boot award and earned himself a call-up to the England squad. He is now the Premier League's all-time top scorer.

SHREEVES, PETER. Though born in South Wales, where his mother was evacuated during World War Two, he was brought up in Islington. After a League career with Reading, he became coach to Charlton Athletic in 1974. Arriving at White Hart Lane a few months later as youth team manager, he gradually worked his way through the ranks to take over from Keith Burkinshaw as manager in June 1984. In his first season in charge, Spurs finished third, the club's only meaningful title challenge since the days of Bill Nicholson, but otherwise he had little success. He moved to Queen's Park Rangers as coach and was hoping to become manager but it went to Trevor Francis instead. He was also assistant to Steve Perryman at Watford before returning to White Hart Lane as Spurs' team manager when Terry Venables moved upstairs to become chief executive. Deprived of Paul Gascoigne's services, he only lasted one season before the most underrated manager in Spurs' modern history was sacked.

SKINNER, JIMMY. Jimmy Skinner served the club as a reserve for Spurs' England international half-backs Arthur Grimsdell and Bert Smith. Signed from his home town club Beckenham in 1919, he had few first-team opportunities until the 1924–25 season when he proved an able deputy for the injured Grimsdell. He continued to provide reliable cover until 1926–27 when he was troubled by a serious ligament injury. However, he also failed to comply with the club's training regulations and was twice suspended for 14 days and when he committed the offence a third time in March 1927 Spurs terminated his contract. He appealed to the Football League but failed to attend the hearing and so automatically lost the appeal!

SKITT, HARRY. Though the majority of Harry Skitt's appearances were at centre-half, he was more than capable of playing in any of the half-back positions. A solid, dependable player, the nearest he came to any honours was in August 1929 when he was chosen as 12th man for the Football League against the Irish League. However, with the emerging talents of Wally Alsford coming to the fore, he was released at the end of the 1930–31 season and joined Chester.

SMALLEST PLAYER. Although such statistics are always unreliable for those playing before the turn of the century, the distinction of being Spurs' smallest player goes to Fanny Walden. One of the smallest players of all time, he described his own measurements as '8st 9lbs and 5ft 2½ in – 5ft 2in after a haircut'. A tricky right-winger and very popular with the crowd, the joke was that he could run through the legs of big full-backs!

SMITH, BERT. Overlooked by the London clubs, Bert Smith had to go to Yorkshire to turn professional with Huddersfield Town. During the First World War he played in the same services' team as Bert Bliss, whose recommendation led to Smith's transfer to Spurs in August 1919. He made his League debut against Coventry City in the opening match of the 1919–20 season and went on to become a first choice half-back for the next eight years. He was a member of the successful team that won the Second Division title in 1919–20 and the FA Cup in 1921. In that season he was one of four Spurs players – the others were Bliss, Dimmock and Grimsdell – who played for England trial games and in 1922 appeared for the Football League against the Scottish League. A strong, defensive player whose relentless tackling caught the eye, he remained with Spurs until May 1930 when he became coach at Northfleet. He later coached in Switzerland.

SMITH, BOBBY. The son of a Yorkshire miner, he was not the prettiest of footballers, but his job was to score goals and this he did with relish. He joined the Chelsea ground staff and made his first-team debut at the age of 17, helping them to avoid relegation. After six years, in which he scored 30 goals in 86 senior games, he joined Spurs for £18,000 in December 1955. In his first five years at White Hart Lane he became the highest scorer in Tottenham history – he exceeded 30 League and Cup goals in each of the four seasons between 1957–58, in which he notched 38 in 40 outings, and 1960–61, the year of the 'double'. For England he scored 13 goals in 15 games before being discarded! However, there were times when Bill Nicholson preferred the subtlety of Les Allen and Smith was left out of the team. At the end of the 1963–64 season Nicholson decided Frank Saul should partner Jimmy Greaves and Smith was allowed to move to Brighton for £5,000. His 18 goals in 31 appearances helped the Seagulls win the Fourth Division championship in his only season with them. He fell out with Brighton over comments in some newspaper articles and was sacked. He later entered non-League football with Hastings United where he played until March 1967

Bobby Smith

and afterwards had a short spell at Banbury United.

SMITH, PERCY. Percy Smith played centre-forward for Preston, scoring 90 goals in 239 League games before joining Blackburn Rovers, where he made 172 appearances at half-back. He began his managerial career at Fleetwood before taking over at Third Division Nelson. He had been manager at Bury for three years before his move to Spurs. At White Hart Lane he spent heavily

157

on reconstructing the side under him, Spurs playing an attractive, short-passing game with the emphasis on attack. Promotion to Division One was gained in 1932–33 and the club finished third the following season before an injury crisis in 1934–35 led to disastrous results and relegation. He made an acrimonious departure, claiming that his team selections had been interfered with by the board.

SMITH, TOM. Tom Smith proved to be one of Spurs' most influential players as the club won its first major honours with the Southern League title and the FA Cup around the turn of the century. One of the fastest wingers in the game, he joined the club from Preston North End and went into the first team straightaway. Adept at sending in high dipping crosses for the forwards to put into the net, Smith himself scored Spurs' second goal in the 1901 FA Cup final replay. It is rather surprising that he never won any representative honours with Spurs, the nearest he got came when he played for an England XI against a Scotland XI to raise funds for the Players' Union. The club were upset when Smith announced his retirement at the end of the 1901–02 season and returned north. A fine all-round sportsman, playing wing three-quarter at rugby and cricket for Maryport, one of his three sons refereed the 1946 FA Cup final.

SOUNESS, GRAEME. Having helped Spurs win the FA Youth Cup in 1970, the tough-tackling midfielder progressed quickly to the fringe of the first team and made his one senior appearance as a substitute for Alan Mullery in Keflavik in September 1971. He grew impatient on the sidelines and returned home to Scotland. Spurs allowed him to move to Middlesbrough for £32,000. At the end of his first season Middlesbrough were promoted to the First Division. In January 1978 he was transferred to Liverpool where he matured into a world-class player. With the Anfield outfit he won almost every honour the game can offer before in July 1984 he turned his attention to Europe and joined Sampdoria of Italy. Returning to Britain as manager of Rangers, he helped to bring honours galore to Ibrox Park, when in April 1991 he returned to Liverpool as manager. After the shock of undergoing major heart surgery, he led them to the FA Cup, the one trophy he failed to capture as a player, before resigning in January 1994.

SOUTHERN ALLIANCE. In 1892 Spurs were invited to be one of the ten founder members of the Southern Alliance and lost only three matches in this league to finish third. The club's officials deemed the campaign unsuccessful and at the end of the season they left.

SOUTHERN DISTRICT COMPETITION. Spurs' only season in this league saw them finish runners-up. The match at Woolwich Arsenal was abandoned after 75 minutes for bad language with Spurs losing 2–1 – the result standing.

SOUTHERN LEAGUE. In 1899–1900 Spurs won the championship after a close struggle with nearest rivals Portsmouth. Their first major success coincided with their move to White Hart Lane. Their old Northumberland Park ground was deemed unsatisfactory for the larger crowds which the club was now attracting. The final straw came when the roof of the stand collapsed during a Good Friday match against Woolwich Arsenal. Spurs were offered a vacant piece of land owned by Charrington Breweries behind the White Hart pub in Tottenham High Road. The first game on the ground was a friendly with Notts County on 4 September 1899, which was won 4–1. In the crunch games with runners-up Pompey, the spoils were shared. Spurs won a Christmas Day clash 3–0, but lost to the only goal of the game in the return in March. During February 1900, Tom Pratt scored a hat-trick in three successive games (Sheppey United 4–1, Brighton United 3–0 and Bedminster 5–2). Only four defeats were recorded during the entire season and they dropped only one point at White Hart Lane. Spurs clinched the championship before only 4,500 spectators against lowly Sheppey United, thanks to goals from Hyde, Pratt and Kirwan.

SPIERS, CYRIL. Joining Aston Villa in 1920, Cyril Spiers was an agile and brave goalkeeper who had just consolidated his position as first choice when he was surprisingly released. He had been injured towards the end of the 1926–27 season and Villa decided he would never play again. However, during the close season, he underwent an experimental operation and arrived at White Hart Lane for a month's trial. Signed permanently, he went on to give Spurs four years' invaluable service. In March 1931 he played in the international trial match, after representing the Football League the previous November. Given a free transfer in May 1933 he joined Wolves where he eventually became assistant manager to Major Frank Buckley. He later became manager of Cardiff City, Norwich City, Crystal Palace and Exeter City before scouting for Leicester City.

SPONSORS. Sponsored by Holsten since the early 1980s, Spurs later signed a four-year deal worth over £4 million from Hewlett Packard. The sponsorship deal took effect from the beginning of the 1995–96 season. From that date all Tottenham Hotspur shirts, tracksuits, training tops and replica kits were emblazoned with the Hewlett Packard logo. Alan Furniss, direct of Hewlett Packard's North European Organisation, commented that Spurs: '. . . reflect the strengths and values that we like to associate with our products . . .'

SPROSTON, BERT. England full-back Bert Sproston had a very short career at White Hart Lane, playing in only nine League matches, yet winning four representative honours. He already had eight caps to his credit when he joined Spurs from Leeds United in October 1936. Having won two more caps and playing twice for the Football League, he was chosen for Spurs' match at Manchester City on 5 November 1938. He did play in the match but not for Spurs. The previous day he was transferred to the Maine Road club having complained he was unable to settle in London. He spent over ten years with City before joining the coaching staff at Bolton Wanderers.

STEEL, BOBBY. The youngest of the three Steel brothers, he made his debut in the club's first League game against Wolves. A regular scorer, he was one of the stars of Spurs' early days in the Football League. A mazy dribbler, he excelled at the passing game and though he played for the Anglo-Scots against the Home Scots, he never won any major honours. He continued to play at inside-left for Spurs until 1913–14 when he moved into the centre-half role vacated by his brother Danny. With the outbreak of war, he continued to show his versatility, playing in any position necessary – centre-forward, outside-left and even left-back. He returned to White Hart Lane when the hostilities were over but with his best years behind him he took up refereeing in the Southern League until his other brother Alex persuaded him to play for Gillingham. An all-round sportsman, he later captained the England bowls team.

STEEL, DANNY. Called up to replace the highly rated Walter Bull early in the 1907–08 season, Danny Steel made the centre-half position his and Spurs were able to part with Bull. Always calm and collected, he was one of three brothers – Alex and Bobby were the others – who played for Spurs. In January 1910, Alex Steel's only appearance for the club, all three played in the match against Bradford City. For the first four years of Spurs' Football League history he and brother Bobby formed the nucleus of the side that found life in the First Division difficult to adjust to. He played in three international trial matches and for the Anglo-Scots against the Home Scots but did not win any representative honours. At the end of the 1911–12 season Steel was released and moved to Third Lanark, but returned to London to finish his career with Clapton Orient.

STEVENS, GARY. Playing for Brighton in the 1983 FA Cup final against Manchester United, Stevens had defended brilliantly and scored a late equaliser that took the game into extra-time and eventually a replay, which the Seagulls lost. Joining Spurs for £300,000 later that summer, he failed to establish himself as a central defender and was switched to full-back. However, it was as a midfield player that he proved highly successful, appearing there in both legs of the 1984 UEFA Cup final and playing for the full England side. Stevens's defensive experiences helped him win the ball and he showed a willingness for joining the attack, which had not been apparent when he played at the back. In March 1985, just as he seemed set to become an England regular, he suffered damaged knee ligaments which kept him out of the team for six months. Thereafter his career was plagued with injury, notably a broken shoulder sustained in an aerial challenge with Wimbeldon's John Fashanu in November 1986 and further knee trouble which dated from a notorious Vinny Jones challenge some two years later. Gary Stevens was loaned to Portsmouth in an effort to prove his fitness and in March 1990 the transfer was made permanent for £250,000. Sadly, however, injuries continued

161

to blight his career and in February 1992 he retired.

STEWART, PAUL. Starting his Football League career with Blackpool, he made rapid progress and signed for Manchester City, who were struggling near the foot of the First Division. Although he could do nothing to prevent City from sliding into the Second Division, 24 goals in 40 League appearances the following season saw him force his way into the England Under-21 side. With Clive Allen moving to France and Nico Claesen returning to Belgium, the Spurs attack looked a little lightweight, so Terry Venables secured Stewart's transfer for a then Spurs record fee of £1.7 million. Suspended for the first few games of the season, he was obviously keen to do well, but had the misfortune to miss a last-minute penalty in his League debut against Manchester United in October 1988. Unfortunately, that seemed to set the pattern and he struggled to justify the fee. Even the acquisition of Gary Lineker failed to provide the boost to the big, bustling Mancunian's modest scoring rate. The turning point in Stewart's White Hart Lane career came in December 1990 in the match against Luton Town. Spurs had two men sent off and Stewart was forced to drop back into midfield. So well did he perform that he played in all but four of Spurs' 1991–92 matches and was called up for the England squad for the first time. With personal pressures he was keen to move north and in July 1992 he signed for Liverpool for £2.3 million. There followed loan spells at Crystal Palace, Wolves and Burnley, but at the time of writing he is still at Anfield.

STOKES, ALFIE. Signed from non-League Clapton in February 1953, Alfie Stokes was one of those players whose records indicate they should have experienced more success in the game than they did. Strong and skilful with a fierce shot he scored on his debut against Bolton Wanderers in a 3–2 win at Burnden Park on 4 April 1953. There was no doubting the Stokes goalscoring pedigree as he netted twice in his only outing for England Under-23s in 1955. His best season for Spurs was 1956–57 when he scored 18 goals in just 21 League outings and on 18 September 1957 he cracked five past Birmingham City's England goalkeeper Gil Merrick in a 7–1 win. That season he played for the Football League and England 'B' but at White Hart Lane he languished in the shadow of Bobby Smith and in 1959 took his talents to Craven Cottage. Later working as a chauffeur, he eventually emigrated to live in Australia.

STORMONT, BOB. Signed from Dundee in the summer of 1897, his aggressive style of play made him a great favourite with the Spurs fans. A member of the side which won the Southern League in 1899–1900, he lost his place during the club's 1901 FA Cup run when player-manager John Cameron preferred to play John L. Jones. Disappointed not to be involved in the club's first major final, he moved to Brentford before taking up refereeing.

SUBSTITUTES. The first ever Tottenham substitute was Roy Low who came on for Derek Possee against Arsenal at White Hart Lane on 11 September 1965. The club had to wait until the seventh game of the 1968–69 season for their first goalscoring substitute – Jimmy Robertson scoring in the 7–0 home win over Burnley. The greatest number of substitutes used in a single season by Spurs under the single substitute rule was 35 in 1984–85 but since 1986–87 two substitutes have been allowed and in 1991–92 69 were used. The greatest number of substitute appearances for Spurs has been made by Paul Walsh who came on during 44 League games with 13 more in cup-ties. It was in 1988–89 that David Howells rewrote the Spurs records on the matter of substitutes with an extraordinary 15 League appearances in the substitute's shirt.

SUPER SPURS. The nickname of the celebrated Tottenham Hotspur side that in 1961 became the first English side of the 20th century to win the 'double' of the FA Cup and the League championship. In the process the team demolished many existing football records, winning 31 games in all and at one point during that memorable season claiming victory in 11 matches in a row. The nickname was still being heard towards the end of the 1960s by which time the Super Spurs had added two more FA Cup victories (1962 and 1967) and another in the European Cup-winners' Cup (1963).

SUSPENSIONS. Tottenham's James Devlin, along with McElhaney, Wilson and Milliken, was suspended for 'acts of insubordination'. Despite this indiscretion he was re-signed for the following season but before it even kicked-off he was again suspended when the club discovered he had also signed for Millwall – in those days Spurs' most fiercest of rivals. He was going to be suspended for the entire season but the situation was resolved in October 1897 when he was transferred to Millwall. James Collins was suspended in November 1896 for 'wilfully disobeying training instructions'. The circumstances of the suspension were never actually publicised but the following month he was sentenced to two months' imprisonment for assaulting the landlord of the Sussex Arms public house in Woolwich.

SUSTAINED SCORING. During the 1930–31 season Spurs were battling with Everton and West Bromwich Albion for the two promotion places from Division Two. Ted Harper, who had joined the club from Sheffield Wednesday, scored 36 goals in 30 appearances to set a League scoring record for Spurs. He scored five on the opening day of the season as Spurs beat Reading 7–1. On 21 March (when he had played 28 games and scored 34 goals) he was injured. In the six games he missed, Tottenham secured only four points and finished third, three points behind West Bromwich Albion.

T

TAIT, SANDY. Known as 'Terrible Tait', for the ferocity of his tackling, he made his name with Motherwell and Preston North End before joining Spurs in the summer of 1899. He gave the club eight years remarkable service, captaining the team in his latter days. Despite his nickname, he was not a dirty player. Hard but fair with a very efficient sliding tackle, he was never booked and was a credit to his profession. His greatest asset was his speed of thought and he always seemed to anticipate situations far quicker than his opponents. A consistent performer, the only representative honour he won during his time at White Hart Lane came in March 1903 in a Scottish international trial match. He remained a regular at Tottenham until 1907–08 when he joined Leyton Orient.

TALLEST PLAYER. It is impossible to say for definite who has been the tallest player ever on Spurs' books as such records are notoriously unreliable. But almost certain to lay claim to the distinction are goalkeepers Joe Nicholls and Erik Thorstvedt who both attained the height of 6ft 4in. Of the outfield players there are a number at 6ft 3in, notably Guy Butters, Harry Clarke, John Lacy and Johnny Metgod.

TAYLOR, PETER. Rejected by Tottenham as a youngster, he went on to become an England international before returning to White Hart Lane in September 1976, a major £400,000 signing from Crystal Palace. A fast-raiding goalscoring winger, he lacked confidence and in a team doomed to relegation in his initial term, he struggled at times. The following season he missed only one game as the club won promotion but then found himself discarded to accommodate Ricky Villa. There followed a series of injuries and so in November 1980 – out of the Spurs side – he joined Orient for £150,000. After playing in the lower divisions and sampling life in the non-League scene he left the game before returning as Steve Perryman's number two at Watford. He is now back as manager at Southend United where his career began in 1971.

TELEVISION. Spurs appeared in the fourth game ever featured on *Match of the Day* when, on 12 September 1964, they went down 3–2 to West Ham United at Upton Park with Jimmy Greaves scoring both Spurs goals.

TESTIMONIALS. For many years Spurs would not grant testimonial matches although quite often they provided the opposition in games for beneficiaries of other clubs. In the early 1970s the policy was changed and Jimmy Greaves was the first player to be rewarded. Spurs beat Feyenoord 2–1 with Greaves grabbing the winning goal. Testimonials were granted for long and distinguished service to the club, but in some instances they were a tribute to players whose careers had met with a tragic end, such as John White and Peter Southey. Bill Nicholson and Keith Burkinshaw also had matches staged for them for bringing success as managers.

TEXACO CUP. The predecessor of the Anglo-Scottish Cup, it was launched in 1970–71 and was for English, Irish and Scottish club sides not involved in European competitions. Spurs only entered in the inaugural season, beating Dunfermline Athletic 4–0 at home and 3–0 away in the first round. In the next round they beat Motherwell 3–2 at home but went down 3–1 at Fir Park to go out 5–4 on aggregate.

THAMES AND MEDWAY LEAGUE. Spurs spent just one season in this league in 1898–99 when they finished third. They started the campaign with six straight wins. The final game of the season saw William Joyce score five goals as Dartford were beaten 9–0.

THOMAS, DANNY. A very popular and friendly player, he made his League debut for Coventry against Spurs in September 1979. He soon established himself in a young talented Coventry team and earned a place in the England Under-21 team. A top-class full-back who could play on either flank, he played twice for the full England team on the tour to Australia in 1983 before Keith Burkinshaw paid £250,000 to take him to White Hart Lane. He played in both legs of the 1984 UEFA Cup final but a serious injury sustained in the match against Queen's Park Rangers in 1987 brought his career to an end, and in January 1988 he announced his retirement after fighting a losing battle to regain fitness. He then qualified as a physiotherapist and in May 1992 returned to the game in that capacity at West Bromwich Albion.

THOMAS, MITCHELL. One of the first footballers to make a career as a professional under the government sponsored Youth Opportunities Scheme, he joined Luton Town as an apprentice just prior to his 17th birthday. Part of David Pleat's outstanding Luton team of the mid-1980s, he followed him to Tottenham in July 1986 for a fee of £275,000. He enjoyed a successful start with Spurs, playing in the 1987 FA Cup final, winning an England 'B' cap against Malta in October of that year and was promoted to the full England squad. However, under new manager Terry Venables his position came increasingly under pressure from new arrivals Gudni Bergsson, Justin Edinburgh and Pat Van Den Hauwe. After being left out of the 1991 FA Cup final, he moved on to West Ham United for £500,000 but could not prevent the Hammers from slipping out of the top flight in 1992.

THOMPSON, ANDY. A fine servant of the club, Andy Thompson only became a first-team regular in the mid-1920s when he moved from inside-forward onto the right wing. He played for the club for 11 years and was a player who, whenever called upon, would never let the club down. During the 1930–31 season, he became surplus to requirements when manager Percy Smith teamed up with Welsh internationals Taffy O'Callaghan and

Willie Davies on the right wing. At the end of the season he joined Norwich City before returning to White Hart Lane, initially as coach, but later doing a variety of other backroom jobs.

THORSTVEDT, ERIK. He had trials for Tottenham Hotspur in December 1984 and also with Queen's Park Rangers, Arsenal and Borussia Moenchengladbach, but it was another four years before he was able to obtain a work permit, allowing Terry Venables to complete his £400,000 purchase from IFK Gothenburg. Drafted in to replace Bobby Mimms, his Spurs career got off to a less than auspicious start when he conceded a 'soft' goal during his Football League debut at home to Nottingham Forest on 15 January 1989, a 2–1 defeat that was televised throughout Europe. Despite this he gradually grew in confidence and became an exceptionally popular goalkeeper. He won an FA Cup winner's medal in 1991 as Spurs defeated Nottingham Forest 2–1. A Norwegian international, his position came under threat from the talented Ian Walker early the following season. In 1992–93 he became the Premier League's first substitute goalkeeper under the new ruling when he came on at half-time following an injury to Walker in the second match of the season. An agile goalkeeper who seems to fill the goal, he is still at White Hart Lane providing cover for the promising Walker.

TICKRIDGE, SID. A strong, determined full-back, Sid Tickridge played for Dartford in 1939–40 and guested for Millwall the following season before making his debut for Spurs in the opening match of the London War League in August 1941. He did not miss a match that season, but further football was limited to service games as he was called up for the Royal Navy. He wasn't able to sign professional forms until 1946 and though he was a regular from 1947, he lost his place to Alf Ramsey and joined Chelsea in March 1951. Taking up coaching, he assisted Millwall before returning to White Hart Lane as youth team trainer.

TOTTENHAM MARSHES. In common with quite a few football clubs, Tottenham's origins go back to a group of cricketers. They formed Hotspur FC in 1882 and played on public pitches at Tottenham Marshes until 1887. That first season was not without its problems. Gangs of bullies frequented the Marshes and taunted the Hotspur members. The players also had to literally fight to keep their pitch. As the team improved it became apparent that they would need a ground of their own. Crowds of up to 4,000 had been assembling on the Marshes to watch them, but of course no gate money could ever be collected.

TOURS. Spurs' first-ever tour was in May 1905 when a lengthy trip to Vienna, Budapest and Prague, taking in seven games, was made. The close season tours abroad were a regular feature of the club's programme and in 1914 nine games were played in Germany, Switzerland, Italy and Austria-Hungary. One game in Germany saw Spurs' goalkeeper 'Tiny' Joyce have his head split open by one umbrella-wielding fan. In 1952 came the club's first-ever tour of Canada. All ten games were won, including two against Manchester United. The tour also included Spurs' highest scoring result in any first team match – an 18–1 victory over the Saskatchewan FA XI with Sid McClellan scoring nine of the goals. The club's longest-ever tour came in the summer of 1976 when they visited Canada, Fiji, New Zealand and Australia.

TRANSFERS. In July 1988 Spurs broke the transfer record when they paid £2 million to Newcastle United for Paul Gascoigne. When he left for Lazio in May 1992, they received £5.5 million, their record fee received. When Bill Nicholson signed Jimmy Greaves from AC Milan in December 1961, it was for £99,999, because he was reluctant to make him the first £100,000 footballer. Mike England cost Spurs a record British fee for a defender when he signed for £95,000 from Blackburn Rovers in the summer of 1966. When Martin Chivers joined Spurs from Southampton in January 1968, the value of the transfer (£125,000) was a British record fee, although Frank Saul, valued at £45,000, moved in the opposite direction. Joining Spurs from Aberdeen for £800,000 in May 1980, Steve Archibald's fee was a record for a transfer between Scottish and English clubs. Spurs' current record signing is Chris Armstrong who cost £4.5 million from Crystal Palace in June 1995.

TRESADERN, JACK. As a player Jack Tresadern started his career with West Ham United and appeared in the first Wembley Cup final in 1923. Following a short spell at Burnley he became player-manager at Northampton Town, but a broken leg brought an end to his playing career. He remained at the County Ground until 1930 when he moved to Crystal Palace in the same capacity. He took up the post of Spurs' manager in 1935, but was not a success. Results were poor and he was unpopular with supporters and club officials. He was not helped by constant rumours of a return for Peter McWilliam as a manager of the club. Knowing the sack was imminent, he made a successful last-minute application for the manager's job at Plymouth Argyle.

TURNER, ARTHUR. Although never officially given the title of Tottenham manager, he fulfilled that position on a number of occasions. One of the founders of Rotherham County he joined Spurs in 1906 as secretary when the club sought to take some of the pressure off manager John Cameron. When the Tottenham board decided not to replace manager Fred Kirkham in 1908, they opted to take control of team affairs themselves. Yet the burden fell on Arthur Turner, who was responsible for the majority of many of the club's most important players being signed. An accountant by profession, he served Tottenham for 43 years until his death in March 1949.

U

UEFA CUP. Formerly known as the Fairs Cup, its name was changed in 1971 when it became the UEFA Cup. Embarking on their first venture into this competition, Spurs beat Icelandic side Keflavik 15–1 on aggregate. The next tie proved much tougher and only a Martin Peters goal separated the sides over the two legs. Rapid Bucharest and Unizale Textile Arad were beaten in the next two rounds before Spurs met AC Milan in the semi-final. The first leg was played at White Hart Lane and after the Italians had taken the lead, it took two strikes from the edge of the area by Steve Perryman to give Spurs a 2–1 win. In the San Siro stadium, Alan Mullery gave the away side the lead after five minutes and though the Italians put Spurs under continual pressure they only scored once. In the final they met Wolverhampton Wanderers over two legs. Martin Chivers scored twice as Spurs won 2–1 at Molineux. In the second leg Mullery scored for Spurs, but Wolves equalised and were probably the better team on the night, but the home side's defence held firm and Spurs won the trophy. The following season Spurs reached the semi-final only to lose on the away-goals rule against Liverpool. In 1973–74 the club reached the final of the competition for a second time, only to lose 4–2 on aggregate to Feyenoord. It was ten years before Spurs participated in the UEFA Cup again, but after victories over Drogheda, Feyenoord, Bayern Munich, FK Austria and Hadjuk

Split, they met Anderlecht in the final. A Paul Miller goal earned Spurs a 1–1 draw in Belgium, whilst it took a late Graham Roberts goal at White Hart Lane to take the tie into extra-time and subsequently a penalty shoot-out. After Anderlecht's first spot-kick was saved, Spurs went into a 4–3 lead. Danny Thomas missed his penalty and it took a magnificent save from Tony Parks to give Spurs the trophy. The last time the club participated in this competition was 1984–85 when they went out in the fourth round 1–0 on aggregate to Real Madrid.

UNDEFEATED. Spurs have remained undefeated at home throughout three League seasons: 1919–20, 1932–33 and 1964–65. The club's best and longest undefeated sequence in the Football League is of 33 matches between 2 January 1932 and 23 September 1933. Spurs' longest run of undefeated Football League matches home and away is 22 between 31 August 1949 and 14 January 1950.

UNITED LEAGUE. Spurs spent three seasons in this competition, finishing as runners-up in their second season in 1897–98. During this season they beat Southampton 7–0 with William Joyce scoring four of the goals.

UNUSUAL GOALS. The Spurs v Huddersfield Town League match on 2 April 1952 provided one of the most controversial goals ever in the Football League. Eddie Baily took a re-taken corner which hit the referee on the back, bounced off back to Baily who chipped it to Len Duquemin, allowing him to score the only goal of the match. Huddersfield protested that Baily had played the ball a second time before it touched another player, so infringing Law 17, but the unsighted referee and the League let the goal stand.

UTILITY PLAYERS. A utility player is one of those particularly gifted footballers who can play in several, or even many, different positions. Two of Tottenham's earliest utility players were Walter Moles and Walter Bull. Moles was an unusually versatile player who was equally at home at half-back or in goal, while Bull appeared in every outfield position! Les Howe was a fine all-round footballer and in his 16 years with Spurs (1930–46) he actually played in every position, even taking over in goal in an emergency. After the mid-1960s players were encouraged to become more adaptable and to see their roles as less stereotyped. At the same time, however, much less attention came to be paid to the implication of wearing a certain numbered shirt and accordingly some of the more versatile players came to wear almost all the different numbered shirts at some stage or another, although this did not necessarily indicate a vast variety of positions. In the modern game Nayim, Samways, Sedgley, Bergsson and Stevens have all been talented enough to wear a variety of outfield shirts.

V

VAN DEN HAUWE, PAT. The son of a Belgian professional goal-keeper, he moved to England at an early age, before signing as an apprentice for Birmingham City in June 1977. Turning professional just over a year later, he made his Football League debut, but it took him a further three years to win a permanent place in the 'Blues' line-up. He alternated between full-back and central defender in a poor Birmingham team and when they were relegated at the end of the 1983–84 season he joined Everton. By the end of his first season at Goodison, he had helped Everton win the Football League title and the European Cup-winners' Cup, reach the FA Cup final and had won his first international cap. Having opted out of National Service, he was ineligible for the country of his birth and chose to play for Wales. Over the next four years he was an Everton regular and by the time of his £575,000 move to Spurs in August 1989, he had won 13 Welsh caps. He returned to Wembley again for an FA Cup final in 1991 and was 'third-time lucky' as Spurs beat Nottingham Forest 2–1. In September 1993 he joined Millwall on a free transfer.

VENABLES, TERRY. England coach Terry Venables was a stylish player with four London clubs and won an FA Cup and League Cup winners' medal during his career. Starting out with Chelsea, he won an FA Youth Cup winner's medal in 1961. He became the

Terry Venables

first player to represent England at five different levels: Schoolboy, Amateur, Youth, Under-23 and Full. His two full caps came when he was a Chelsea player. After 237 League and Cup appearances for the Stamford Bridge club, he moved to Tottenham Hotspur for £80,000 in May 1966. In his first season with Spurs, he won an FA Cup winners' medal against his former club Chelsea, but overall he failed to win over the critical White Hart Lane fans. He made 139 League and Cup appearances for Spurs, scoring nine goals before his transfer to Queen's Park Rangers for £70,000 in June 1969. He spent five years at Loftus Road before moving on to Crystal Palace. His playing career was near its end and after only 14 games he retired to become coach at Selhurst Park under Malcolm Allison. In June 1976, when Allison left, Venables became manager and in his first season in charge led the Eagles to promotion from Division Three. In 1978–79 Palace were Second Division champions. On entering the top flight, Venables signed Spurs' present manager Gerry

Francis from Queen's Park Rangers for £450,000 but in their second season in the First Division they began badly and in October 1980 he resigned after a boardroom row. Immediately joining Queen's Park Rangers as manager he led them to the FA Cup final in 1982 and the Second Division title in 1983. In May 1984 he received a huge offer to manage Barcelona. With former Spurs striker Steve Archibald leading the attack, Barcelona won the Spanish League title at the end of his first season in charge. The following year they reached the European Cup final but lost on penalties to Steaua Bucharest. They finished runners-up to Real Madrid in the League in 1986–87 and after only four games of the following season he resigned. He returned to England to manage Spurs and bought a large interest in the club. He took Spurs to the 1991 FA Cup final where they beat Nottingham Forest 2–1. Public disclosure of the club's precarious financial situation meant that he was unable to go and strengthen his squad. Along with computer millionaire Alan Sugar, he masterminded a takeover at Spurs, working hard to clear the club's debt. In May 1991 he became chief executive as Peter Shreeve returned to White Hart Lane. His contribution at Tottenham was always full of incident and culminated in public conflict with Sugar in 1993. His eventual dismissal provoked fierce protest among his many devoted fans, but in 1994 he was appointed England coach.

VICTORIES IN A SEASON – HIGHEST. In the 1919–20 season Spurs won 32 of their 42 League fixtures to win the Second Division championship, the highest in the club's history. In 1960–61 they won 31 of their 42 Division One matches to win the championship with 66 points, eight points ahead of Sheffield Wednesday.

VICTORIES IN A SEASON – LOWEST. Spurs' poorest performance was in 1914–15 when they won only eight matches out of their 38 League games and finished bottom of the First Division. In modern times their worst record was in 1993–94 when, despite winning 11 of their 42 fixtures, they finished 15th in the table, thanks mainly to 12 fixtures ending all-square.

VICTORY INTERNATIONALS. Spurs had a number of players represent their country during the Victory and wartime internationals. The most notable were Ron Burgess who made ten appearances for Wales, Ted Ditchburn who played twice for England and Vic Buckingham who also made two appearances for England. Arthur Grimsdell was the only Spurs player to represent his country in the Victory internationals of 1919, playing twice against Scotland and scoring two goals.

VIDEOS. Tottenham Hotspur have produced a number of videos in conjunction with the BBC, the most notable being an official history of the club.

VILLA, RICARDO. He was little known to British fans when, valued at £375,000, he accompanied Osvaldo Ardiles to White Hart Lane in July 1978. He had made two appearances as a substitute for Argentina in the 1978 World Cup finals, when they won the trophy. He scored on his Spurs debut at Nottingham Forest, but had difficulty finding a regular role at White Hart Lane. Taking longer to settle in a strange country, the big bearded Villa was also hampered by injuries. However, he became a folk-hero with his display in the 1981 FA Cup final. Having scored with a spectacular 30-yard shot against Wolves in the semi-final replay, he had a very poor game in the drawn Centenary final and shuffled his way back to the dressing-room in tears after being substituted. Manager Burkinshaw stuck by him for the replay and was rewarded in spectacular fashion when, with the score at 2–2 (Villa had netted the first goal), he set off on a mazy run past Caton, Ranson and Caton again before his strong right-foot shot beat the despairing Corrigan – it was without doubt one of the greatest individual goals ever seen at Wembley. He came on as substitute during the 1982 Milk Cup final but missed the FA Cup final that year as Burkinshaw decided it was better to omit him in view of the strong feelings surrounding the Falklands conflict. In June 1983 he joined Fort Lauderdale Strikers in America and later played in Colombia before taking up coaching back home in Argentina.

W

WADDLE, CHRIS. One of the most skilful of modern-day players, he started his career with Newcastle United, who picked him up from local Northern League club Tow Law Town in the 1980 close season. Under the guidance of manager Arthur Cox he made rapid progress at St James Park and along with Peter Beardsley and Kevin Keegan helped the Magpies gain promotion in 1984. Called up the following season for his first England cap against the Republic of Ireland on 26 March 1985, he remained a regular member of the squad for the next six seasons. Spurs signed him in July 1985 for £590,000 and after scoring two goals on his debut in a 4–0 home win over Watford, he struck up a fine understanding with Glenn Hoddle. He enjoyed an excellent second season at White Hart Lane, playing in 39 Football League games in a campaign when Spurs finished third in Division One and reached the 1987 FA Cup final only to lose unexpectedly to Coventry City. He spent much of the following season sidelined with heel and hernia problems, but came back strongly in 1988–89 in a new creative midfield role to be ever-present and top scorer with 14 Football League goals, taking Spurs to sixth place after being rooted to the foot of the table in November. At the end of that season Spurs received an offer of £4.25 million from French champions Olympique de Marseille. It was hard to turn down such a bid, but the final decision was left to Waddle and he accepted the oppor-

Chris Waddle

tunity. In three seasons with the French club he won three League championship honours and reached the final of the 1991 European Cup when Marseille lost on penalties to Red Star Belgrade after a dreadful 0–0 draw. Playing probably his last game in an England shirt against Turkey in October 1991, he had scored a paltry six goals in his 62 international appearances. Released by Marseille in July 1992, he returned to England with another major move to Sheffield Wednesday. He ended his first season with the Owls as the Football Writers' Player of the Year and at the time of writing the Hillsborough club continue to benefit from his silky skills.

WALDEN, FANNY. One of the smallest players of all time, Frederick 'Fanny' Walden was a right-winger whose intricate dribbling skills made him very popular with the public. His first Football League club was Northampton Town, for whom he scored a hat-trick on his Southern League debut from the centre-forward position! He was signed by Northampton from Wellingborough Town, Walden's home-town club. That was in 1909 and four years later Spurs offered a record £1,700 for Walden's transfer and he made his debut against Woolwich Arsenal on 19 April 1913. A firm favourite with the White Hart Lane crowd, he won his first England cap in April 1914. After the war he was one of the stars of the Tottenham team that won the Second Division title in 1920, but missed the 1921 FA Cup final victory over Wolves due to a cartilage injury. He returned to the side early the following season and won his second cap against Wales in March 1922 – but for the intervention of the First World War he would surely have won far more. A Northamptonshire county cricketer and later first-class umpire, he returned to Northampton for the 1926–27 campaign, his last playing season.

WALKER, IAN. Son of the former Norwich City and Everton manager, Mike Walker, he had been on Associated Schoolboy forms at Queen's Park Rangers before joining Spurs' trainee staff. He helped the Spurs youth team win the FA Youth Cup in 1990, but due to the consistency of Erik Thorstvedt he was unable to get a game in the first team and was loaned out to Oxford United. He made his Football League debut in a 1–1 draw at the Manor Ground against Wolverhampton Wanderers. Such was his talent that he made his debut for the England Under-21 team against Wales in December 1990 before his Spurs debut in an end of season game at Norwich in April 1991. With the advantage of first-hand coaching by former England 'keeper Ray Celmence, Ian Walker is clearly a player with a great future in the game, having appeared in Terry Venables' England squads.

WALSH, PAUL. A skilful, ball-playing forward, his natural talent was clear at an early age. He began with Charlton Athletic and won Under-21 and full England caps after a move to Luton Town in July 1982. He was the PFA's Young Player of the Year in 1984, the year of his big money move to Liverpool. He was expected to succeed Kenny Dalglish, but despite a European Cup final in 1985, a League title in 1986 and a League Cup final in 1987, he was too often left on the fringes. He became Terry Venables' first major signing when he joined Spurs for £500,000 in February 1988. He soon became a great favourite of the White Hart Lane crowd, but was unable to deliver the quantity of goals his talents deserved. As a result, he spent too much time on the substitutes' bench and after an incident with Ray Clemence he joined Queen's Park Rangers on loan with a view to a permanent transfer. It did not work out and he returned to Spurs before joining Portsmouth as a £400,000 slice of Darren Anderton's transfer to White Hart Lane in May 1992. After playing an integral role in Pompey's spirited bid for promotion to the Premier League, he signed for Manchester City in March 1994 for £700,000. It proved an inspired move by Brian Horton as he linked well with Rosler and Beagrie and scored vital goals to lift City clear of danger. He later returned to Fratton Park.

WALTERS, CHARLIE. An amateur with Oxford City, he played one game as a guest for Spurs during World War One before signing professional forms for the club in April 1920. One of the fastest players on Spurs' books, he came in for Charlie Rance during the FA Cup-winning season and was in the team that beat Wolves in the final. A speedy centre-half, he kept his place for the next two seasons before losing it to Harry Skitt and moved to Fulham before finishing his career with Mansfield Town.

WALTERS, SONNY. Born in Edmonton, he played for Walthamstow Avenue before joining Spurs just before the end of the Second World War. He took a while to establish himself in the side and it was only in April 1949 that he won the fight with Freddie Cox for the outside-right spot. A goalscoring winger, he still linked well in the 'push and run' system, blending in perfectly with Alf Ramsey and Bill Nicholson. He won a Second Division championship medal in 1949–50 and a League championship medal the next season. Unfortunate to play in the same international era as Matthews and Finney, his only representative honour was to play for England 'B' against Holland in 1950. He gave great service to Spurs before leaving in July 1957 for Aldershot, where he played for a couple of seasons.

WALTON, JOE. A fast, direct outside-right, Joe Walton first played for Preston North End when he was just 17 years old. After five years at Deepdale he moved to Spurs and made his debut in the opening match of the 1903–04 season against Woolwich Arsenal. He did not manage to win international recognition, though he did play in three trial matches. Offered the maximum wage to re-sign in April 1909, he refused the offer and joined Sheffield United.

WANT, TONY. A stalwart of Spurs' successful Football Combination side of the late '60s, he was unlucky to be with the club at the same time as players like Cyril Knowles and Joe Kinnear. An England youth international, he never quite made the breakthrough from reliable deputy to regular first-teamer, though he never let anyone down when he did get a chance. A quick, aggressive left-back, he was obviously too good for contin-ual reserve football and in June 1972 was allowed to move to Birmingham City for £50,000. He spent six years at St Andrews before finishing his career in the United States.

WAR. Tottenham have lost a number of players fighting for their country. During the First World War, Jim Fleming, who scored a hat-trick in Paris on his senior debut for the club, was killed in action in Belgium. 'Darkie' Tull, who was possibly the first coloured player to appear in the Football League, was also killed in action as was Findlay Weir. Ed Lightfoot, who rendered the club valuable service in 1914–15 when Spurs were badly hit by players joining the forces, was eventually called up himself and was killed in action in France during July 1918.

WAR FOOTBALL. In spite of the outbreak of war in 1914, the major football leagues embarked upon their planned programme of matches for the ensuing season and these were completed on schedule at the end of April the following year. The season saw the club finish in last place in the First Division. Arsenal's Henry Norris set out to form the London Combination, but there was opposition from the Football League, who threatened expulsion for any club playing a wartime match not organised by the League. Eventually the Football Association intervened and clubs were allowed to organise their own competitions provided there was no interference with war work. In 1918–19 as well as appearing in the London Combination, Spurs also played two matches in the Victory Cup. In contrast to the events of 1914, once war was declared on 3 September 1939, the Football League programme of 1939–40 was immediately suspended and the government forbade any major sporting events, so that for a while there was no football of any description. For the 1939–40 and 1940–41 seasons, Spurs competed in the Football League South and League War Cup with the extra competition in 1940–41 of the London War Cup which was arranged as the League competitions provided an insufficient number of fixtures. In 1941 Spurs were 'expelled' from the League after a dispute over the fixtures and so played in the London War League and London War Cup. The dispute was resolved by the start of the following season and for the rest of the war Spurs played in the Football League South and League War Cup, except 1945–46 when the FA Cup replaced the League War Cup.

WARD, RALPH. Turning professional with Bradford Park Avenue, Ralph Ward gave two outstanding performances in the 1935–36 FA Cup matches against Spurs and within a month the club had signed the full-back who would serve them well for the next ten years. Throughout the war years he captained the club, but by October 1945 he realised his playing days were coming to an end and he became assistant golf professional at Bush Hill Golf Club.

WATSON, JOHN. Everton's regular left-back for two-and-a-half years, injury cost him his place midway through the 1901–02 season. Even though he recovered the position, he was persuaded to join Spurs in May 1902 but spent the first two years at White Hart Lane as cover for Harry Erentz and Sandy Tait. A solid and dependable full-back, it wasn't until Erentz left for Swindon that Watson emerged as the club's regular right-back. He held the spot for two years before losing it to John Chaplin.

WELLER, KEITH. He spent two years with Spurs as cover for the first choice wingers Jimmy Robertson and Cliff Jones, but despite acquitting himself admirably when he did deputise, he was unable to claim a regular place. In June 1967 he moved to Millwall for £18,000 and dropped back into midfield to form a most effective partnership with his former Spurs colleague Derek Possee. He later moved to Chelsea and though he was a member of their triumphant European Cup-winners' Cup team of 1971, he didn't really settle at Stamford Bridge and moved to Leicester City for £100,000. At Filbert Street he really flourished and made his England debut in May 1974, the first of four caps. At the end of the 1977–78 season he went to America to play for New England Teamen and later Fort Lauderdale Strikers.

WEST STAND. Built at a cost of £4.25 million it was, at the time, the most expensive structure ever to be added to a League ground. The stand was formally opened by Sir Stanley Rous before the game against Wolverhampton Wanderers on 6 February 1982. They were the ideal visitors, having been the opposition for White Hart Lane's very first League game in 1908. They went down 6–1 with Ricky Villa grabbing his first hat-trick in England.

WHATLEY, BILL. Another of the fine players discovered through the club's Welsh scouting network, Bill Whatley joined the professional staff at White Hart Lane in 1932 after developing through Hayward Sports and Northfleet. Replacing the injured Cecil Poynton in Spurs' promotion season, he became the club's first choice right-back until the outbreak of war. In 1938 he won two caps for Wales, but at the start of the 1939–40 season he lost his place to Bill Nicholson. An ankle injury forced him to retire in 1947, but he was appointed chief scout and helped to discover Harry Clarke and Mel Hopkins.

WHITE, JOHN. He played for Alloa Athletic for two years before joining Falkirk for £33,300 in September 1958 and within a year was in the Scotland team, making his international debut against West Germany in May 1959. A year later he joined Spurs for £20,000 and made a goalscoring debut at Sheffield Wednesday. His style was delicate and subtle and the Spurs fans took a while to understand and accept him. But soon they christened him 'The Ghost' as he popped up from nowhere to receive or make a telling pass. All Spurs' triumphs over the next three seasons owed plenty to White's input. His talents continued to be seen on the international stage and he won 18 full caps in his time with Spurs. He also played for the Football League against the Irish League in October 1960 and for Scotland against the Scottish League twice.

John White

By the summer of 1964, with Blanchflower retired, he was set to assume extra midfield responsibility. But on 21 July, while practising alone at Crews Hill golf course, Enfield, he was caught in a thunderstorm and sheltered under an oak tree. Lightning struck and at 27 John White was dead.

WHITE, ROY. Whilst many players had their careers curtailed by World War Two, Roy White would probably never had made his mark in the game had it not been for the hostilities. Evacuated from Dunkirk, he spent several hours in the water following the sinking of his boat. Blinded for a time, he was forced to spend a period in hospital where he met Jock McKay who recommended him to Spurs. Invited to watch Spurs play Arsenal, he was surprisingly asked to make up the numbers and thereafter played regularly throughout the war. At the end of the Second World War, Spurs offered him professional terms, but he returned to Liverpool to continue his studies.

WHITE HART LANE. The site was a neglected nursery which the brewers Charrington had bought from a firm called Beckwiths. There were still greenhouses and sheds on the land, but the brewery intended to build houses there. Charrington's also owned the nearby White Hart Inn. An added convenience of the ground was that the club's headquarters were already at 748 High Road next to the public house. Tottenham's first game there was a friendly against First Division Notts County. A crowd of over 5,000 saw Spurs win 4–1. by the end of that 1899–1900 season Tottenham were Southern League champions. In 1908 Tottenham were elected to the Second Division of the Football League. It took the club only one season to gain promotion to Division One and to celebrate this event they officially opened their new West Stand in September 1909. The designer was Archibald Leitch. It seated 5,000 with room for 4,000 in the covered paddock in front. A large mock-Tudor gable displayed the words 'Tottenham Hotspur F & A Co Ltd' in ornate lettering. In 1910 the famous ball and cockerel symbol, which was synonymous with Tottenham Hotspur thereafter, was added to the top of the gable. Also in 1910 both open end banks were doubled in size and soon after the East Side cover taken down, so that the terraces there could also be expanded. The ground now had a capacity of 40,000. When the First World War broke out the ground was taken over for use as a rifle range, opened by the founder of the Scout movement, Lord Baden-Powell. During the first few years after the war, the Paxton Road End was covered, paid for by the profits of Tottenham's victorious FA Cup run of 1921 and then in 1923 an almost identical stand was built at the Park Lane End. In 1936 Spurs decided to build a stand on the uncovered East Side. In design it appeared to be one of the largest stands in the country, although it was essentially a standard Archibald Leitch design placed on an extra pedestal of terracing. On 5 March 1938, Tottenham's highest attendance of 75,038 saw Sunderland win 1–0 in the FA Cup sixth round. For many years the White Hart Lane pitch had drained badly and was consequently very muddy in winter. During the summer of 1952 it was completely reconstructed. Underneath the pitch the old Beckwith Nursery greenhouses were found. They were removed and a new filter bed installed. Throughout the club's successful period in the '60s and '70s the only major change at White Hart Lane came between 1962–65 with the conversion of the rear half of both end stands to hold 3,000 seats each. In 1979 it was decided to rebuild completely the West Stand. Investing in a new structure which would give White Hart Lane the potential for everyday use, the most spectacular modern stand built in England was opened on 6 February 1982 by Sir Stanley Rous. In the mid-'80s Tottenham spent £450,000 on safety work at the ground, including the installation of 13 closed-circuit television cameras. In 1986 the club replaced their undersoil heating system at a further cost of £100,000.

WILLIS, ARTHUR. Arthur Willis played for Finchley before joining Spurs as an amateur in 1938. He made his debut during the war and after signing professional, played regularly in one of the full-back positions until September 1947 when he lost the right-back spot to Sid Tickridge. He did not get back into the team until early in the 1950–51 season when an injury to Withers gave him a chance for a prolonged spell at left-back. He ended the season with a League championship medal and in October 1951 collected an England cap against France. Quick and sharp, Willis was a good footballing full-back but similar to Withers and over the next three seasons they vied continually for the first-team position. Willis stayed with Spurs until September 1954 when he left to join Ron Burgess at Swansea Town.

WILSON, CHARLIE. Though Charlie Wilson scored a hat-trick in his League debut at South Shields on 20 September 1919, he spent the whole of his first season as reserve to Jimmy Cantrell, but his seven goals in 12 games helped Spurs to the Second Division title. With Cantrell coming to the end of his career, he vied with Alex Lindsay for the next two seasons to establish himself as Cantrell's successor. However, when Herbert Chapman, manager of Huddersfield Town, made a bid for Wilson's services, Spurs decided to let him go. He was top scorer for Huddersfield in 1924 and 1925 when the Yorkshire side won successive League titles, but was left out the following season when they made a bid for a third title. Moving to Stoke City he was the Potters' leading scorer in four of his five full seasons with them.

WITHERS, CHARLIE. He played with Tottenham Juniors and Finchley before signing professional forms with Spurs in October 1947. A hard-tackling full-back he made his League debut against Barnsley the following March, taking over from Vic Buckingham midway through the 1949–50 season. However, in 1950–51 he lost his place to Arthur Willis but re-established himself the following season and was in and out of the side until he retired. In over 200 senior appearances for the club, Charlie Withers scored only two goals. For the FA Cup fourth round tie with Preston North End in January 1953, Spurs had an injury crisis and he was pressed into service as an emergency left-winger. He responded with both goals as Spurs drew 2–2.

WOODWARD, VIVIAN. Despite remaining an amateur throughout his long career, Vivian Woodward was one of the outstanding footballers of his generation. An architect by profession, he began his career with Chelmsford City but in 1901 he accepted an invitation to join Spurs, although business commitments restricted his appearances until 1902–03. By the end of his first full season he had made his debut for the England team, scoring twice against Ireland. Tall, slim and elegant, Woodward went on to score 28 goals in 23 appearances (21 of them as a Spurs player) for the full England team and also played 67 amateur internationals for England and the United Kingdom, captaining the team that won the Olympics in 1908 and 1912. Woodward scored Spurs' first Football League goal and was leading scorer in the promotion-winning team. Having the unique distinction of being a Tottenham director, he was vastly respected by team-mates and opponents alike and was often referred to as 'Sir'. He shocked not only Spurs but the whole football world when in 1909 he resigned as both player and director. He surprised Spurs even further during the 1909–10 season when he returned to the game as a Chelsea player. He remained with them until the outbreak of World War One and served as a director at Stamford Bridge between 1922 and 1930.

WORST START. The club's worst ever start to a season was in 1912–13. It took 14 League games to record the first victory of the season, drawing just three and losing 10 of the opening fixtures. The run ended with a 1–0 success over Newcastle United at White Hart Lane on 23 November 1912 and though the club lost their next match 4–1 at Oldham, they were unbeaten in their next five fixtures and ended 17th in the First Division.

X. In football X traditionally stands for a draw. The club record for the number of draws in a season was in 1968–69 when they managed 17 draws out of 42 matches.

XMAS DAY. There was a time when football matches were regularly played on Christmas Day, but in recent years the game's authorities have dropped the fixture from their calendar. The last time Spurs played on Christmas Day was in 1958 when they went down 2–1 to West Ham United at Upton Park. One of the most memorable Christmas Day games was in 1952 when Spurs beat Middlesbrough 7–1 with Les Bennett grabbing four of the goals. Four years later they beat Everton 6–0.

Y

YORATH, TERRY. An often under-appreciated member of the great Leeds side of the late 1960s and early 1970s, the rugged blond Welsh international won 59 caps. Keith Burkinshaw signed him from Coventry for £275,000 in August 1979 to add a bit of steel to a midfield that boasted the talents of Ardiles, Hoddle and Villa. Possessing a shrewd grasp of tactics and an accomplished distribution he performed admirably for a season but after suffering a series of injuries early in 1980–81 he was unable to reclaim a regular place in the face of competition from Graham Roberts and that summer moved to Vancouver Whitecaps. He later returned to these shores to launch a successful career in coaching and management, culminating in the position of full-time manager for Wales.

YOUNG, WILLIE. Signed from Aberdeen for £120,000 in September 1975, Willie Young became a cult figure at White Hart Lane, although he had his faults. Well over six feet tall, he was a hard-headed centre-half that few centre-forwards were able to get the better of. However, by mid-1976–77, after some disappointing displays, the huge Scot was dropped by new boss Keith Burkinshaw. It was still surprising when Spurs agreed to transfer Young to Arsenal for £80,000, but he was keen to link up again with Terry Neill at Highbury. He spent four years at Highbury and played in three successive FA Cup finals between 1978 and 1980 before assisting Nottingham Forest and Norwich City.

YOUNG PLAYER OF THE YEAR. The Professional Football Writers' Association Young Player of the Year has been won by Tottenham players on two occasions. These are:
1980 Glenn Hoddle
1988 Paul Gascoigne

YOUNGEST PLAYER. The youngest player to appear in a first-class fixture for Tottenham Hotspur is Ally Dick, who played in the First Division match against Manchester City (home 2–0) on 20 February 1982 when he was 16 years 301 days old. The youngest player to appear in the Premier League is Spurs' Andy Turner who was 17 years 145 days old when he played against Southampton (away 0–0) on 15 August 1992. He also became the youngest scorer when he scored in Spurs' 2–1 victory over Everton at White Hart Lane on 5 September 1992.

YOUTH CUP. Tottenham Hotspur have won the FA Youth Cup on three occasions. The aggregate scores of these two-legged finals have been:
1970 Tottenham Hotspur 4 Coventry City 3 (after two replays)
1974 Tottenham Hotspur 2 Huddersfield Town 1
1990 Tottenham Hotspur 3 Middlesbrough 2

Z

ZENITH. Few fans will argue over which moment has been the finest in the club's history. The appointment of Bill Nicholson as manager paved the way for the formation of arguably the greatest English club side since the war when, in 1961, they became the first team to do the Cup and League double this century.